22

READINGS ON

CRIME AND PUNISHMENT

Other titles in the Greenhaven Press Literary Companion Series:

American Authors

Maya Angelou
Stephen Crane
Emily Dickinson
William Faulkner
F. Scott Fitzgerald
Robert Frost
Nathaniel Hawthorne
Ernest Hemingway
Herman Melville
Arthur Miller
Eugene O'Neill
Edgar Allan Poe
John Steinbeck
Mark Twain
Walt Whitman
Thornton Wilder

American Literature

The Adventures of Huckleberry Finn
The Adventures of Tom Sawyer
Black Boy
The Call of the Wild
The Catcher in the Rye
The Crucible
Death of a Salesman
Fahrenheit 451
A Farewell to Arms
The Glass Menagerie
The Grapes of Wrath
The Great Gatsby
Of Mice and Men
The Old Man and the Sea
One Flew Over the Cuckoo's Nest
Our Town
The Pearl
The Scarlet Letter
A Separate Peace
To Kill a Mockingbird

British Authors

Jane Austen
Joseph Conrad
Charles Dickens
J.R.R. Tolkien

British Literature

Animal Farm
Beowulf
Brave New World
The Canterbury Tales
Frankenstein
Great Expectations
Hamlet
Heart of Darkness
Jane Eyre
Julius Caesar
Lord of the Flies
Macbeth
The Merchant of Venice
Othello
Pride and Prejudice
Romeo and Juliet
Shakespeare: The Comedies
Shakespeare: The Histories
Shakespeare: The Sonnets
Shakespeare: The Tragedies
A Tale of Two Cities
Tess of the d'Urbervilles
Wuthering Heights

World Authors

Fyodor Dostoyevsky
Homer
Sophocles

World Literature

All Quiet on the Western Front
The Diary of a Young Girl
A Doll's House

THE GREENHAVEN PRESS
Literary Companion
TO WORLD LITERATURE

READINGS ON

CRIME AND PUNISHMENT

Derek C. Maus, *Book Editor*

David L. Bender, *Publisher*
Bruno Leone, *Executive Editor*
Bonnie Szumski, *Series Editor*

Greenhaven Press, Inc., San Diego, CA

Every effort has been made to trace the owners of copyrighted material. The articles in this volume may have been edited for content, length, and/or reading level. The titles have been changed to enhance the editorial purpose. Those interested in locating the original source will find the complete citation on the first page of each article.

Library of Congress Cataloging-in-Publication Data

Readings on Crime and punishment / Derek C. Maus, book
    editor.
        p.   cm. — (The Greenhaven Press literary
    companion to world literature)
    Includes bibliographical references and index.
    ISBN 0-7377-0234-6 (pbk. : acid-free paper). —
ISBN 0-7377-0235-4 (lib. : acid-free paper)
    1. Dostoyevsky, Fyodor, 1821–1881. Prestuplenie i
nakazanie. I. Maus, Derek C. II. Series.
PG3325.P73 R43   2000
891.73'3—dc21   99-055780
                                                            CIP

Cover photo: Scala/Art Resource

Copyright ©2000 by Greenhaven Press, Inc.
PO Box 289009
San Diego, CA 92198-9009
Printed in the U.S.A.

I have too often had to produce thoroughly bad things through haste, writing to schedule, etc. [Crime and Punishment], however, has been written unhurriedly and with enthusiasm.

—Fyodor Dostoyevsky on
Crime and Punishment
in a letter to his publisher
from September 1865

Contents

Chapter 1: The Critical Reception of *Crime and Punishment*

Chapter 2: The Composition and Narration of *Crime and Punishment*

FOREWORD

*"'Tis the good reader that
makes the good book."*

Ralph Waldo Emerson

The story's bare facts are simple: The captain, an old and scarred seafarer, walks with a peg leg made of whale ivory. He relentlessly drives his crew to hunt the world's oceans for the great white whale that crippled him. After a long search, the ship encounters the whale and a fierce battle ensues. Finally the captain drives his harpoon into the whale, but the harpoon line catches the captain about the neck and drags him to his death.

A simple story, a straightforward plot—yet, since the 1851 publication of Herman Melville's *Moby-Dick*, readers and critics have found many meanings in the struggle between Captain Ahab and the whale. To some, the novel is a cautionary tale that depicts how Ahab's obsession with revenge leads to his insanity and death. Others believe that the whale represents the unknowable secrets of the universe and that Ahab is a tragic hero who dares to challenge fate by attempting to discover this knowledge. Perhaps Melville intended Ahab as a criticism of Americans' tendency to become involved in well-intentioned but irrational causes. Or did Melville model Ahab after himself, letting his fictional character express his anger at what he perceived as a cruel and distant god?

Although literary critics disagree over the meaning of *Moby-Dick*, readers do not need to choose one particular interpretation in order to gain an understanding of Melville's novel. Instead, by examining various analyses, they can gain numerous insights into the issues that lie under the surface of the basic plot. Studying the writings of literary critics can also aid readers in making their own assessments of *Moby-Dick* and other literary works and in developing analytical thinking skills.

The Greenhaven Literary Companion Series was created with these goals in mind. Designed for young adults, this unique anthology series provides an engaging and comprehensive introduction to literary analysis and criticism. The essays included in the Literary Companion Series are chosen for their accessibility to a young adult audience and are expertly edited in consideration of both the reading and comprehension levels of this audience. In addition, each essay is introduced by a concise summation that presents the contributing writer's main themes and insights. Every anthology in the Literary Companion Series contains a varied selection of critical essays that cover a wide time span and express diverse views. Wherever possible, primary sources are represented through excerpts from authors' notebooks, letters, and journals and through contemporary criticism.

Each title in the Literary Companion Series pays careful consideration to the historical context of the particular author or literary work. In-depth biographies and detailed chronologies reveal important aspects of authors' lives and emphasize the historical events and social milieu that influenced their writings. To facilitate further research, every anthology includes primary and secondary source bibliographies of articles and/or books selected for their suitability for young adults. These engaging features make the Greenhaven Literary Companion Series ideal for introducing students to literary analysis in the classroom or as a library resource for young adults researching the world's great authors and literature.

Exceptional in its focus on young adults, the Greenhaven Literary Companion Series strives to present literary criticism in a compelling and accessible format. Every title in the series is intended to spark readers' interest in leading American and world authors, to help them broaden their understanding of literature, and to encourage them to formulate their own analyses of the literary works that they read. It is the editors' hope that young adult readers will find these anthologies to be true companions in their study of literature.

INTRODUCTION

Fyodor Dostoyevsky's *Crime and Punishment* is well established within the body of so-called classic works of world literature. This groundbreaking work has made an impact well beyond the borders of the time and space in which it was originally created. The novel has been translated into several dozen foreign languages, and new editions of the work continue to be published.

The central plot of *Crime and Punishment* is amazingly simple for a novel of over five hundred pages in length: A young man kills an old woman and her sister during a robbery attempt and then spends the rest of the novel trying not to get caught. Although the plot seems simple, the number of critical views represented in this volume is testimony that it is not.

One of the most interesting aspects of *Crime and Punishment* is that, although written in the nineteenth century, it is exceptionally modern in its approach. Dostoyevsky's novel manages to reach deeper into the mind of a troubled individual than any book that preceded it. The seeming simplicity of the plot may therefore not be a flaw. Rather, it is indicative of the fact that Dostoyevsky's very intent was to create a study of the psyche within a character like Raskolnikov, not a murder mystery.

The essays in this volume approach *Crime and Punishment* from a number of different angles. Some attempt to psychoanalyze the characters in the book, arguing that Dostoyevsky was writing about mental illness in a time when mental illness was poorly understood. Others sift carefully through the language that Dostoyevsky uses in creating the novel, looking for patterns that associate characters with philosophical ideas or social movements. Still others see the strong role of religion in Dostoyevsky's personal life and look at the novel in terms of its possible statement of faith. The wonder of *Crime and Punishment* is that it gives admittance to all of these theories and more without resistance.

Crime and Punishment is, in the end, a moral book. From Dostoyevsky's own comments on its composition and by examining his personal beliefs, it is clear that Dostoyevsky believed in the redemptive teachings of the Russian Orthodox Church. Whether the reader agrees with Dostoyevsky's ending is ultimately irrelevant, for the book's crowning achievement is that Raskolnikov's struggle with his evil impulses, his acting out on those impulses, and his ultimate decision on how to redeem himself remain meaningful today.

FYODOR DOSTOYEVSKY: A BIOGRAPHY

In late 1821 a son, Fyodor Mikhaylovich Dostoyevsky, was born to Mikhail Andreyevich Dostoyevsky, a Moscow doctor, and Marya Fyodorovna Dostoyevskaya. The nation he was born into was entering a tumultuous period that would last for almost a hundred years, culminating with the Bolshevik Revolution of 1917 that put an end to the Russian Empire.

In many ways the young Fyodor Dostoyevsky grew up at the same time as the growing radical sentiment that would eventually culminate in the Russian Revolution. His public life and his career as a writer can be seen as an ongoing debate with the philosophies represented by this new spirit. Dostoyevsky went from being a somewhat brash, youthful socialist, to being a staunch defender of the Russian Orthodox Church and one of the most recognizable voices of the conservative Slavophile movement. His lifetime of affiliations runs almost the entire range of possibilities available to a member of the privileged classes in nineteenth-century Russia.

BIRTH AND CHILDHOOD

The Dostoyevskys already had one child at the time of Fyodor's birth, a son named Mikhail who had been born a little less than two years before. This brother would be a lifelong friend and companion to Fyodor, first as a schoolmate and later as a business partner. Their relationship was far closer than the ones Fyodor had with his other siblings. The family eventually grew to include two younger brothers, Andrei (born in 1825) and Nikolai (born in 1831), and three younger sisters, Varvara (born in 1822), Vera (born in 1829), and Alexandra (born in 1835). Vera had a twin sister, Lyubov, at birth, but this child lived only a few days.

Mikhail Andreyevich Dostoyevsky was a doctor at the Mariinsky Hospital for the Poor, a profession that brought him social status if not a great deal of actual monetary reward. He had achieved entry into the Russian privileged class through his civil service at the hospital. This kind of upward social mobility had become possible because of the establishment of the "Table of Ranks" in 1722 by Peter the Great. With this table Peter had reformed the Russian nobility by making it possible to earn one's way into the aristocracy by acts of service to the state. Prior to this, a noble title was available only through birth into a family that was already a part of the nobility. Peter's table set up a list of ranks for civil servants and military officers that were parallel and equal to the old aristocratic titles. Peter's reforms went a long way to expanding the upper class in Russia, but they were unpopular among the more traditional elements of Russian society that viewed the new "meritocracy" as an unwelcome innovation.

Although accounts of Dostoyevsky's father vary somewhat, he was apparently both very caring toward his family as well as given to periods of severe cruelty and ill temper. He insisted on an education for his children and had them schooled (or instructed them himself) from a young age not only in the Bible and in Russian Orthodox dogma but also in history, literature, and philosophy. He even placed his sons in private schools to avoid the brutal beatings that were so common in public schools (and which have been documented by countless Russian writers). Even at age seventeen, though, Fyodor seems to have been somewhat ambivalent toward his father, writing the following in a letter to his brother:

> I pity poor father! What a strange character he has! How much he had to suffer! I am so sorry that I could weep, because I can do nothing to console him. And you know, Papa has absolutely no idea about the world; he has lived in it for fifty years and his opinion of people is just what it was thirty years ago.[1]

Dostoyevsky's mother was in turn the great love of his young life. A gentle, intelligent, and devoutly religious woman, Marya Dostoyevskaya was extremely sickly during much of her later life. In addition to being weakened by pregnancy for a good portion of the fifteen-plus years between Fyodor's birth and her death, she suffered from a number of serious illnesses during this time. The degree of the young Dostoyevsky's attachment to his mother can be seen in this letter, which she sent to her from boarding school at the age of thirteen:

> When you left, dear Mama, I started to miss you terribly, and
> when I think of you now, dear Mama, I am overcome by such
> sadness that it's impossible to drive it away, if only you knew
> how much I would like to see you and I can hardly wait for
> that joyous moment. Every time I think of you I pray to God
> for your health.[2]

The love of his mother, as well as the considerable attention
given to him by the family's nurse, Alyona Frolovna, tempered
the harshness of his father's discipline and provided most of
the fond memories that Dostoyevsky took from his childhood.

ADOLESCENCE AND EDUCATION

Fyodor and his older brother, Mikhail, went through school
together throughout their early years. Their father taught
them Latin and religion at home for many years, and they attended several different boarding schools in Moscow between 1833 and 1837. They switched schools often, as their
father regularly became dissatisfied with the methods of
their various teachers. Nevertheless, both brothers managed
to receive a relatively thorough education that at least partially satisfied their intellectual curiosity. Young Fyodor read
widely in history, philosophy, and literature, not only Russian but also European (especially French and German).

In addition to their formal education, the boys received a
different kind of schooling through the summers they spent
between 1831 and 1837 on the family's newly acquired estate
in the village of Daravoe. This piece of land, purchased by
Dostoyevsky's father in 1831, gave Fyodor a firsthand look at
peasant life in Russia. He not only played with and became
friends with the children of serfs at Daravoe, but he also witnessed the hardships and brutality of peasant life. Much of
Dostoyevsky's understanding and sympathy for the serfs and
other nonprivileged Russian classes stems from the summers he spent in Daravoe. His subsequent experiences in St.
Petersburg and in Siberia would reinforce his sense of ideological (if not necessarily social) fraternity with this group.

For all of his attempts at enlightening his sons, Dostoyevsky's father was not entirely pleased with the direction that
their education was taking as of 1837. He did not share their
love for subjects like literature and philosophy and decided
to enroll them in a boarding school in St. Petersburg. This
school would prepare them for the more "practical" profession of military engineering and would subsequently lead to
admission in the Academy of Military Engineers.

Before they departed for St. Petersburg, though, their mother succumbed to tuberculosis and exhaustion from repeated pregnancy and childbirth, dying at thirty-seven years of age. Her death exacted a heavy emotional toll on the adolescent Fyodor. Further troubling to him was the death, from injuries sustained in a duel, of his literary idol Aleksandr Pushkin. Pushkin's writings were favorites of the impressionable young Dostoyevsky, and Fyodor famously stated to his father that he would have been in mourning for Pushkin were it not for the fact that he was already mourning for his mother.

In this state, the grieving Dostoyevsky set off for school in St. Petersburg with his father and brother. During a stop on the way there, they witnessed a drunken government courier savagely beating a horse. Dostoyevsky was powerfully struck by this episode and refers to it in his notebooks. The scene he witnessed here would crop up almost thirty years later as part of a dream Raskolnikov has in *Crime and Punishment*, a telling demonstration of Dostoyevsky's ability to recall and utilize personal incidents, even from his early life, in his writing.

He continued his exemplary academic performance in his studies despite the fact that he was separated from both his brother Mikhail and his father before the end of 1839. Because of his excellent schoolwork at the preparatory school, Fyodor was admitted to the Academy of Military Engineers in early 1838. Mikhail was denied admission because of minor health problems and subsequently moved away to Estonia. This marked the first time the brothers had been separated for a significant period of time since Fyodor's birth.

At roughly the same time, his father began a process of mental and physical decline in the wake of his wife's death. He became even more harsh and unpredictable in his later years, damaging the already strained relationship with Fyodor even further. He died under mysterious circumstances in the summer of 1839 after having moved to Daravoe. The sketchy details surrounding his death include a largely debunked story that he was killed by his own serfs, but the actual details of his death are not definitively known. By almost all accounts, though, he was verging on insanity by the time he died.

Despite his troubles, Fyodor continued his studies at the Academy and eventually graduated in 1843. In the intervening years, however, he became friends with a number of other young St. Petersburg students and began an increasingly active (and expensive) social life there. Beginning a cycle that would last much of his life, he became dependent on financial assistance from both Mikhail and his younger sister Varvara, who had married a rich widower named Karepin in 1840. He lived an extravagant and expensive lifestyle, spending nights on the town carousing and associating with many of the brightest young sons of aristocrats in St. Petersburg society. He also read voraciously, spending a considerable amount of what little money he had on the latest books.

Upon his graduation in 1843, he entered the St. Petersburg Engineering Command, a largely bureaucratic military job that provided him with little in the way of either intellectual stimulation or financial support. As a means of supplementing his income, Dostoyevsky used his broad education to translate books by Balzac and George Sand from French into Russian. The pay from these projects was small, but the experience made him decide that writing was his true calling. At age twenty-two he resigned his commission from the army in order to devote himself fully to the composition of his first novel, the work that would become *Poor Folk*.

DOSTOYEVSKY AMONG THE INTELLIGENTSIA

Poor Folk, a novel about a love affair between two working-class city dwellers, was moderately well received among the progressive critics of the time. Realistic, sympathetic writing about the life of the lower classes was something that the newer, more radical Russian critics were readily embracing at this time, and Dostoyevsky's novel fit the bill well. In more mainstream critical circles, though, it was panned for its unusual subject matter and form, traits that would be hailed in Dostoyevsky's work later in his career.

Largely because of the subject of *Poor Folk*, but also because of his personal political sympathies, Dostoyevsky made the acquaintance of Vissarion Belinsky, one of the leading lights of the more radical and socially conscious wing of the Russian literary scene. Belinsky praised the young Dostoyevsky's work and encouraged him to continue in his art, thereby establishing a direct mentoring relationship that would continue for the next two years.

Belinsky's political beliefs were very much in line with those of Dostoyevsky, who likewise fancied himself a friend of the downtrodden and supported the end of serfdom in Russia. In 1845 Dostoyevsky wrote to his brother Mikhail that Belinsky "is extremely well disposed toward me and seriously sees in me a public vindication of his ideas."[3] However, Belinsky was an avowed atheist and was hostile to the Russian Orthodox religion in which Dostoyevsky was raised and which remained a central part of his life. The impossibility in reconciling this antireligiosity with the desire to improve the social and economic status of the poor made Dostoyevsky's relationship to the radical left troublesome throughout the rest of his life.

As a result of the relative success of *Poor Folk*, Dostoyevsky made the acquaintance of many of the up-and-coming talents in Russian literature, including Ivan Turgenev. Although the two never became particularly close friends (and actually eventually became bitter rivals as Dostoyevsky's conservatism emerged), they discussed the craft of writing extensively during this early stage of their respective careers. Dostoyevsky was mixing personally with many of the thinkers and writers who would shape the thought of the coming decades. Even after he broke with the progressives, Dostoyevsky's experiences in this group serve as models for characters and ideas.

In the phase of his career that followed the publication of *Poor Folk*, Dostoyevsky returned to a more traditional style of writing, one heavily influenced by romanticism and the stories of the great Russian writer Nikolay Gogol. He published *The Double* and *Mr. Prokharchin* in 1846, followed by a series of short stories that appeared in *Notes from the Fatherland*, a left-leaning journal published by the reformist critic Nikolay Nekrasov.

Because of their less radical subject matter, Dostoyevsky was widely (and inaccurately) accused of abandoning his principles by many of the same critics who had praised *Poor Folk*. None of these works was particularly successful, either in critical or commercial terms, which caused Dostoyevsky to rely heavily on the financial support of his brother. Even Belinsky refused to soften his unkind words against the new direction he saw in Dostoyevsky's work. This led to a disintegration of the formerly close relationship between himself and Dostoyevsky.

During this period, Dostoyevsky had begun associating with a group of radical intellectuals led by Mikhail Butashevich-

Petrashevsky, known as the Petrashevsky circle. This group read and discussed foreign and Russian socialist works and favored such politically dangerous topics as the abolition of serfdom or the relaxation of the governmental censorship of literature. Dostoyevsky himself became an outspoken and very visible figure in this group. He also convinced his brother Mikhail to take part in the meetings.

In 1848 a number of socialist uprisings took place in Germany and elsewhere in Europe. Fearing a similar turn of events in Russia, the government of Nicholas I resolved to crack down on potentially revolutionary groups. Dostoyevsky, along with his brother and thirty-two other men associated with the Petrashevsky circle, was arrested in April 1849 and imprisoned in the Peter and Paul Fortress in St. Petersburg. Mikhail was released not long after (having had little real contact with the group), but Fyodor and most of the others were held for more than six months, at the end of which fifteen of the prisoners (including Dostoyevsky) were sentenced to execution for allegedly plotting to overthrow the government.

Little evidence exists that the group was planning any sort of a coup, especially since they hardly had the numbers or the resources to do so. They were convicted largely on the basis of having read and circulated a letter by Belinsky that accused the Russian government of being immoral because of its continued support of serfdom.

For more than a month, Dostoyevsky prepared himself to die, not knowing that Nicholas I had commuted the sentence to four years' hard labor in Siberia. The czar, wishing to make an example of these men (without turning them into martyrs), allowed the plans for the execution to proceed right up until the moment when the prisoners were actually to be shot, at which point he would spare their lives officially in a demonstration of his merciful nature. The men were paraded out to the execution ground in freezing weather and were actually lined up against the wall where they were to be shot before the courier from the czar arrived with the pardon. He described the scene as follows in a letter to his brother written the very same day:

> Today, December 22, we were taken to Semyonov Square. There we were all read the death sentence, allowed to kiss the cross, had sabers broken over our heads and our pre-death attire put on (white shirts). Then three people were stood

against the stakes for the carrying out of the execution. I was sixth in line, people were summoned by threes, consequently I was in the second row and had no more than a minute left to live. I remembered you, brother, and all of your family; at the last moment you, only you were in my mind, only then did I realize how much I love you my dear brother!... Finally a retreat was sounded, the ones tied to the stake were led back, and it was announced that His Imperial Majesty was granting us our lives.[4]

In his later reminiscences of the experience, Dostoyevsky claims that several of the men who were seemingly fated to die with him went insane because of the stress of the ordeal. Dostoyevsky himself used the firsthand experience of near-execution in several of his later works, most notably *The Idiot.*

IMPRISONMENT AND EXILE

After their reprieve, the prisoners were sent off to a prison camp in Omsk in Siberia. Before he arrived in Omsk, though, Dostoyevsky was given a copy of the New Testament by the wife of a former prisoner at a transit camp. It was the only book he was allowed to take with him to the camp. He later claimed that this book helped him endure the horrific privations and abusive conditions he endured in the camps. In a lengthy letter he wrote to his brother Mikhail upon his release from the camp, Dostoyevsky described some of the hardships:

[The deputy commandant] always came in riding drunk (I never saw him sober), would pick on a sober prisoner and flog him on the pretext that the latter was as drunk as a cobbler. . . . I spent the entire four years in prison without going out, behind walls, and went out only for work. The work that fell to us was difficult, of course not always, and on occasion I exhausted myself in bad weather, in the wet, in the slush, or in the wintertime in unbearable cold. Once I spent about four hours at special work when the mercury had frozen, and it was perhaps 40 degrees below freezing. My foot got frostbitten. We lived in a heap, all together in one barracks.[5]

The four years he spent in the camps served as material for several works, including *The House of the Dead* and the epilogue of *Crime and Punishment.* It was also during his time in the camps that his epilepsy first manifested itself, beginning a long period of health problems that would last until the end of his life.

When released from penal service in Omsk, Dostoyevsky was still not entirely free. He was required to serve in the military at a Siberian outpost in Semipalatinsk, a small town in the Kirghiz steppes. He immediately began trying to re-gain his rights as a citizen (as well as trying to get back to western Russia), an effort that was greatly aided by his friendship with Baron Alexander Vrangel. Vrangel was a twenty-one-year-old civil service officer from St. Petersburg who, along with Mikhail Dostoyevsky, provided the impov-erished Fyodor with financial assistance and friendship dur-ing these troubled years.

In Semipalatinsk, Dostoyevsky also met the woman who would eventually become his first wife, Marya Dmitrievna Isaeva. She was still married to a local government official when they met, but they struck up a friendship and soon began an affair that lasted for several months until the Isaevs moved away, much to Dostoyevsky's chagrin. How-ever, his grief was not destined to last long, as Marya's hus-band died within months of their departure. Marya returned to Semipalatinsk, and she and Dostoyevsky were married eighteen months later.

With his new wife, and through the intercession of his friend Vrangel, Dostoyevsky redoubled his efforts to return to his former life and finally succeeded in 1859, when the authorities allowed him to resign from the military and move to Tver, a city in the provinces of northwestern Russia between Moscow and St. Petersburg.

RETURN TO ST. PETERSBURG

However, Dostoyevsky was determined to return to St. Pe-tersburg and, partly due to the more liberal attitude of the new czar, Alexander II (he succeeded Nicholas I in 1855), he was granted permission to do so in December 1859. During this year, he began publishing things that he had written during the past nine years, including a number of short sto-ries and the longer tale *The Village of Stepanchikovo and Its Inhabitants*. Soon after returning to St. Petersburg he also published the first part of his fictionalized memoir of life in the prison camps.

At this time Dostoyevsky and his brother Mikhail set into motion plans to start a new literary journal, a notion that they had first formulated during the time of Fyodor's exile in Semipalatinsk. This new journal, called *Time* (*Vremya*), was intended to occupy the political space between the more radical journals like Nekrasov's *Notes of the Fatherland* and the conservative publications that had long dominated Russian literary criticism. *Time* began publication in 1861 and the journal immediately published Dostoyevsky's novel *The Insulted and the Injured* in serial form.

Between the hard lessons learned during his imprisonment and a growing disaffection with the politics of his former radical colleagues, Dostoyevsky's beliefs had become more conservative in the decade that had passed. Although he still sympathized with the plight of the serfs, his tolerance for revolutionary ideas had diminished greatly and *Time* provided him with a mouthpiece through which he could criticize the radicals. This mixture of social concern and traditional beliefs made him popular with a large portion of Russian society, ranging from emancipated serfs to members of the old Russian nobility. Dostoyevsky's position was further improved by the ascension of Alexander II to the throne, since this czar was known for his more enlightened policies, such as abolishing serfdom in 1861.

As Dostoyevsky's journalistic career took off and his writing career resumed its initial promise, his marriage to Marya began to fall apart. The couple became more and more estranged as Dostoyevsky's influence and popularity increased, and by summer of 1862 they were hardly a couple anymore except in name. His public life as a literary figure consumed so much of his time that he rarely saw his wife for long stretches of time.

With *Time* firmly established and under the financial and editorial care of Mikhail, Dostoyevsky went on a three-month trip to Europe, most notably to London, where he witnessed firsthand the Western world that stood in opposition to what Dostoyevsky treasured in his Slavic homeland. Dostoyevsky had increasingly thrown his political allegiance behind a faction that advocated a return to Russian values that existed before the reforms of Peter the Great. They believed that Peter's innovations, which were intended to make Russian culture and government more like western Europe, had been harmful to the traditions of Russian culture, which they believed to be superior to those of the West. This group, known widely as the Slavophiles, were strongly rooted in the tenets of the Russian Orthodox Church and usually supported the rule of the czars. Even at this stage of his life, Dostoyevsky was more liberal than most Slavophiles in regard to his beliefs about social justice and responsibility for the poor, but these ideas were not in conflict with those of Orthodox Christianity. What he saw in most of the West during this visit was not only a lack of compassion and concern for the poor but also a substitution of economic materialism for the religious values he held so dear.

Upon his return to St. Petersburg, he wrote a highly critical memoir of his travels called *Winter Notes on Summer Impressions*, which was published the next spring in *Time*. At around the same time, the journal had begun publishing the work of a young woman named Apollonaria Suslova, the daughter of a recently freed serf with whom Dostoyevsky would strike up an on-again, off-again amorous relationship that lasted for the better part of the next four years.

In May 1863 *Time* was banned by the government because of a misunderstanding about its political position, and the Dostoyevsky brothers were forced to petition the government yet again, this time for permission to resume publication. In the mean time, Fyodor asked Mikhail for another loan, the purpose of which was to provide him travel funds to visit the West again. His motive for leaving at this time was largely to pursue Suslova, who had moved to Paris. He stopped off in Germany briefly, where he gambled (and lost) heavily. Nearly broke, he managed to make it to Paris, where he met up with Suslova. They traveled together from there to Germany again and then on to Italy. However, their romance never fully materialized and Dostoyevsky returned to St. Petersburg in October and continued the attempts to resume his journalistic career in order to set his troubled finances in order.

With *Time* still under government ban, the brothers started a new monthly publication called *Epoch* (*Epokha*), which immediately began serial publication of Dostoyevsky's next major novel, *Notes from Underground*. During the composition of this book, Dostoyevsky suffered personal loss again when his wife died of tuberculosis in April.

Perhaps even more importantly, his beloved brother and business partner Mikhail died of liver failure in July. He was overworked and exhausted from the considerable effort of keeping *Epoch* afloat and simultaneously managing the finances of his family and his free-spending brother. Dostoyevsky wrote to his younger brother Andrei immediately after Mikhail's death about the circumstances of Mikhail's decline:

> Last year the journal [*Time*] was prohibited. That struck him like a bolt out of the blue and suddenly produced such a mess in all his affairs, threatened such a catastrophe, that he spent

all last year in constant alarm, agitation and fears. . . . Large
debts had been accumulated. We began publishing a journal,
spent money, but couldn't get by without debts. . . . Suddenly
everything collapsed, and with the prohibition of the journal,
credit collapsed too. The year was a hard one and our
brother's health suffered severely.[6]

Dostoyevsky continued to edit *Epoch* after Mikhail's
death. Both the articles contained in it and his own fictional
works began more and more to confront the Russian radical
critic Nikolay Chernyshevsky and his beliefs directly. Dostoyevsky especially targeted the ideas contained in Chernyshevsky's book *What Is to Be Done?*, which had become
something of a bible for the radical segment of the Russian
intelligentsia. Chernyshevsky was one of the foremost leftist
writers of the 1860s and 1870s and spent a considerable
amount of time in prison or in exile for the ideas contained
in his writings. *What Is to Be Done?* is a utopian novel that
advocates the overthrow of the czar and the establishment of
a democratic state. Chernyshevsky was heavily influenced
by German and French socialist writers, a fact that made
him even less desirable to Slavophiles like Dostoyevsky.

Both *Notes from Underground* and *Crime and Punishment*
are, in large measure, attempts to discredit the philosophy of
Chernyshevsky and his followers. Characters like "the underground man" (the unnamed protagonist of *Notes from Underground*), Raskolnikov, and Ivan Karamazov in *The Brothers Karamazov* are, for Dostoyevsky, "polluted" by the ideas
of Chernyshevsky and his followers. From this point onward,
Dostoyevsky's works and his personal philosophy were dominated by a more explicitly conservative stance against the
liberalism and Westernization represented by the radical
Russian left. He felt a strong allegiance with Alexander II,
whom he felt to be in many ways the model of an enlightened
autocratic ruler, and defended him from the threat he cor-
rectly perceived in those who sided with Chernyshevsky.

CRIME *AND* PUNISHMENT AND BEYOND

As 1865 arrived, Dostoyevsky was at a critical stage in both
his personal life and his development as an author. He took
care of Mikhail's family after his brother's death and broad-
ened his involvement with the rest of the family (since he
was now its oldest male member). Editing *Epoch* demanded
his full attention and left him little time for his own fiction.

Furthermore, he engaged in a very purposeful yet fruitless search for another wife, proposing unsuccessfully not only to Apollonaria Suslova but also to three other women between 1865 and late 1866. When *Epoch* shut down publication in early 1865 for lack of funding, Dostoyevsky was desperate for money. In July he signed a contract with Fyodor Stellovsky, a wealthy but somewhat disreputable publisher. This contract required him to produce a new novel by November 1866. If Dostoyevsky did not meet this obligation, Stellovsky would immediately acquire all the rights to his prior works.

Dostoyevsky took the money that he had received from Stellovsky for the rights to publish a collected edition of his prior writings and departed for Germany. He wrote copiously while there, especially while gambling in Wiesbaden, where he drafted *The Drunkards*, which would later become *Crime and Punishment*. However, he also became even more addicted to gambling and carried on his unsuccessful courtship of Suslova. He offered the early drafts and outlines of *The Drunkards* to several journals, but most of his old colleagues in the leftist press would not accept this work, riddled as it was with his new, more conservative point of view. He even burned the manuscript of a nearly completed version of the novel at one point, although he fortunately left the notebooks intact. He finally was able to sell the rights to the *Russian Messenger*, a journal published by Mihkail Katkov, one of the most outspoken Slavophiles in Russia at the time.

Dostoyevsky wrote a letter to his old friend Baron Vrangel from Wiesbaden in which he described both his economic state and his new writing project:

> And meanwhile, if I'm given time to finish it, the story that I'm working on now may be the best thing I've written. O my friend! You wouldn't believe what torture it is to write to order. And it's even materially unprofitable: the weaker a thing is, the more the price decreases. But what am I to do: I have debts of 15,000 [rubles], while last year at this time I wasn't a kopeck in debt.[7]

He stopped in Copenhagen to visit Vrangel (and to borrow some money) for two weeks late in 1865, after which he returned to St. Petersburg. Not long after his return, he and Suslova ended their relationship once and for all. With this painful experience still in his recent memory, *Crime and Punishment* began its year-long serial publication in the *Russian Messenger*. Numerous critics have noted that his emotional state in the wake of his break with Suslova had a profound effect on the mood of the novel. He wrote feverishly, adapting passages from the copious notebooks that he had been writing in throughout the past year. He met his obligation to Katkov concerning *Crime and Punishment*, often providing chapters for the journal only days before deadlines. The achievement of the novel is all the more remarkable given the conditions under which its author was working as he created it.

The matter of the novel he owed to Stellovsky, though, was unresolved as the summer of 1866 drew to a close. Dostoyevsky had been working on drafts of a novel that he intended to be an exploration for the motivations behind his growing addiction to gambling and a purgation of the memories of his affair with Suslova. He realized, though, that he could not finish this novel and keep writing *Crime and Punishment* at the same time, so he hired a stenographer to help him with the transcription of his manuscript for *The Gambler.* This nineteen-year-old woman, Anna Grigorievna Snitkina, not only helped him meet his contractual obligations but also became Dostoyevsky's second wife in the process.

She was, unlike the other women he had proposed to since his first wife's death, a devoutly religious and conservative young woman, bearing many similarities to Sonya Marmeladova from *Crime and Punishment.* It is important to note, however, that her effect on the development of that character is minimal at best, since she did not meet Dostoyevsky until October 1866, at which point *Crime and Punishment* was almost completed. He wrote of her in a letter to his friend Apollon Maikov:

> It is true that Anna Grigorievna has proven to be a stronger and deeper person than I had thought her to be, and at many instances she has simply been my guardian angel; but at the same time there is much of the child and the twenty year-old in her that is good and natural and inevitable, but I hardly possess the strength or ability to respond to it.[8]

He proposed to her in November, after the completion of *The Gambler* and they were married three months later.

FOUR YEARS ABROAD

Despite Dostoyevsky's aversion to much of what western Europe represented, the couple spent their first four years of marriage living for short periods of time in Germany,

Switzerland, and Italy. Much of this "second exile" (as Dostoyevsky himself called it on occasion) was due to the continuing debt that he incurred as he attempted to care for his extended family and live the life to which he had become accustomed. While living in Germany, Dostoyevsky gambled heavily once again, losing most of the money the couple had taken with them and forcing them to pawn many of their personal belongings. He also managed, though, to write fairly prolifically during this time, beginning the notes on his next great novel, *The Idiot.* Having moved from Dresden to Geneva in 1867, Dostoyevsky continued to work on drafts of *The Idiot,* which was serialized in 1868, again in the *Russian Messenger.* While in Geneva, Dostoyevsky's first child was born, a daughter named Sofia, after a favorite niece of Dostoyevsky's and like the heroine of *Crime and Punishment.* The child was born in February 1868 but sadly lived only three months.

After the infant's death, the couple moved to Italy, where Dostoyevsky apparently found some elements of Western life that he could hold in esteem. The spirituality and vitality of Italian life held great appeal to Dostoyevsky and stood in contrast to the mercantilism and capitalism he had witnessed in England and Germany. During the nine months that he lived there, he finished *The Idiot* and also wrote a short piece called *The Eternal Husband,* which was published early in 1870.

The couple moved to Dresden, where their second child, a daughter named Lyubov, was born in September 1870. Dostoyevsky had indicated in letters to friends that he was working on a massive book intended to rival the recently published *War and Peace* by Leo Tolstoy in both scope and quality. Although he never finished this work, alternately titled, *The Atheist* and *The Life of a Great Sinner,* he drew on the mountain of preliminary notes he made for this work in creating his remaining novels.

He sent the first part of *The Devils* (also known as *The Possessed* or *Demons*) to the *Russian Messenger* for publication in late 1870 and finished it over the course of the next year and a half. It was his most vehemently conservative work to date, condemning the ideas of the revolutionary anarchist Sergey Nechayev and his followers. The work stirred up controversy and angry condemnations among the leftists as well as earning critical praise from the Slavophiles. He sent a copy directly to Alexander II with a letter that clearly stated its meaning for him:

> It is almost a historical study, in which I have sought to account for the possibility of such monstrous phenomena as the Nechayev movement occurring in our strange society. In my view, it is not an accidental or isolated phenomenon. It is a direct consequence of the profound estrangement of Russian education from the native, home-grown foundations underlying Russian life.[9]

This novel represents the completion of Dostoyevsky's shift to the side of the Slavophiles, and he was one of the most prominent anti-revolutionary voices for the remaining years of his life.

Dostoyevsky went on one final gambling spree in Wiesbaden, Germany, in April 1871, after which he made a difficult yet apparently genuine promise to kick the habit. The family scraped together enough money to make it back to St. Petersburg and find lodging, just in time for their first son, Fyodor, to be born in July 1871.

THE FINAL DECADE

Over the course of the next few years Dostoyevsky worked on two more novels: *A Raw Youth*, which came out in 1875, and *The Brothers Karamazov*, which was published in 1879–1880. He also began publishing a feature, entitled *The Diary of a Writer*, in a new conservative weekly journal called the *Citizen*. As the journal's handpicked editor, he was given relatively free reign to voice his opinion on political, social, and religious affairs, and he quickly established a large and loyal readership. By this stage of his life, Dostoyevsky's conservatism was firmly entrenched, and *The Diary of a Writer* was largely composed of his arguments in favor of the Slavophile position in all matters. Still, Dostoyevsky was not simply parroting a politically popular position in this regard. In fact, *The Diary of a Writer* was discontinued when Dostoyevsky's critical assertions about the role of the secret police in Russian society clashed with the more harsh views of the *Citizen*'s publisher, Prince Meshchersky.

The Diary of a Writer was revived by Dostoyevsky as an independent publication in 1876, and it was an important mouthpiece for the Slavophile movement in its battle against the increasingly active revolutionary movements in Russia. Dostoyevsky continued as editor until late 1877, when he gave it up due to his increasingly fragile health (he had begun suffering from chronic emphysema) and his desire to concentrate on the writing of what would be his final great work, *The Brothers Karamazov*. Anna went through the painstaking labor of proofreading, editing, and collecting the individual features of *The Diary of a Writer* together into a new edition and sold them by subscription in order to make money while Dostoyevsky wrote.

The Dostoyevskys had another son, Alyosha, in 1875, but he suffered from epilepsy like his father and died in 1878. Alyosha's death heavily influenced the writing of *The Brothers Karamazov*. The "hero" of the novel, if it can be said to have one, is the youngest of the brothers, Alyosha Karamazov, who undergoes a difficult education in the ways of the world in the course of the novel. If only as a character in a novel, Alyosha was granted a measure of eternal life through his depiction in this remarkable epic work of fiction, hailed by many as Dostoyevsky's masterpiece. Furthermore, as part of his effort to get over the grief of Alyosha's death, Dostoyevsky sought out Father Ambrose, a famed Orthodox ascetic from whom he sought spiritual counsel. Ambrose provided a model for Father Zosima, the saintly cleric of *The Brothers Karamazov*.

The Brothers Karamazov tries to demonstrate the ways in which Russia deviated from what Dostoyevsky believed was its true path. The several failed attempts that were made on the life of Alexander II during the last years of the 1870s demonstrated that this deviation was dangerous for the status quo in Russia with which Dostoyevsky had allied himself. Perhaps the most memorable quote from the novel is reminiscent of the main theme of Raskolnikov's article in *Crime and Punishment*. Spoken by Ivan Karamazov, the line reads "If God does not exist, then everything is permitted." Dostoyevsky did not intend this to be a justification for the increasingly violent times of the late 1870s, rather he wanted it to be representative of the false premises of the revolutionaries, whom he identified with the character of Ivan. Dostoyevsky, like most of the Slavophiles, was certain of the existence of God. He believed that the denial of God's existence was the foremost fault of the revolutionaries, a denial that could conceivably even lead a son to justify the murder of his own father.

Dostoyevsky's already poor health deteriorated notably during 1880. When he delivered a rousing speech at a ceremony for the dedication of a monument to Pushkin in Moscow in May of that year, it was to be the last great moment of his public life. His speech called on the Russian people to unite themselves toward the goal of making Russia the foremost nation of Europe, not by imitating western Europe but by presenting a new Slavic model for the rest of the world to follow. His conciliatory message, palatable both to Slavophiles and Westernizers, caused even some of his old political rivals, including Turgenev, to congratulate him afterward.

Even though he had a number of projects that he still wanted to complete, Dostoyevsky's declining health made it difficult for him to work for sustained periods of time. He still envisioned the next volume of his planned masterwork (of which he conceived *The Brothers Karamazov* to be the second volume), but he did not live to see more than a first installment completed.

He had contracted severe emphysema late in 1880 and suffered a ruptured lung during a heated argument with his sister Vera in January 1881. He died two days later. After an enormous funeral procession, he was buried by order of the czar in the cemetery at the St. Alexander Nevsky Monastery in St. Petersburg, one of the most revered sites in the Russian Orthodox Church. Czar Alexander II, whom Dostoyevsky had defended and admired so greatly, also died early in 1881, killed by a bomb-throwing assassin. This action signaled an intensification of the conflict between revolutionary and reactionary forces in Russia. Alexander II's assassination marked the violent beginning of almost forty years of bloodshed, culminating in the revolutions of 1905 and 1917 and the civil war that followed.

Anna Dostoyevskaya outlived her husband by almost four decades. Her diaries and a volume of reminiscences of her life with the great writer were published after her death in 1918.

NOTES

1. Joseph Frank and David I. Goldstein, eds., *Selected Letters of Fyodor Dostoyevsky.* New Brunswick, NJ: Rutgers University Press, 1987, p. 12.

2. David Lowe and Ronald Meyer, eds., *Fyodor Dostoyevsky: Complete Letters Volume One, 1832–1859.* Ann Arbor, MI: Ardis, 1988, p. 17.

3. Frank and Goldstein, *Selected Letters of Fyodor Dostoyevsky*, p. 31.

4. Lowe and Meyer, *Fyodor Dostoyevsky: Complete Letters Volume One, 1832–1859*, p. 178.

5. Lowe and Meyer, *Fyodor Dostoyevsky: Complete Letters Volume One, 1832–1859*, pp. 186–87.

6. David A. Lowe, ed., *Fyodor Dostoyevsky: Complete Letters Volume Two, 1860–1867*. Ann Arbor, MI: Ardis, 1989, pp. 125–26.

7. Lowe, *Fyodor Dostoyevsky: Complete Letters Volume Two, 1860–1867*, pp. 177–78.

8. Frank and Goldstein, *Selected Letters of Fyodor Dostoyevsky*, p. 249.

9. Frank and Goldstein, *Selected Letters of Fyodor Dostoyevsky*, p. 369.

CHARACTERS AND PLOT

LIST OF CHARACTERS

Due to inconsistencies in transliterating the Cyrillic alphabet into Latin letters, the names of many of Dostoyevsky's characters are spelled differently in various translations of *Crime and Punishment* and in critical works that discuss the novel. Also, the characters in the novel often refer to each other using diminutives (shortened forms of first names, usually used only with close friends, family relations or children) and using first names and patronymics (middle names derived from the name of one's father; these are used when addressing someone in most informal social situations). Russians generally only use last names in addressing each other in very formal situations, which explains why some characters' last names are not given in the novel. The guide below is intended not only to clarify any possible confusion that might arise from these variant spellings, but also to give some insight into the associations that arise from the names that Dostoyevsky has given some of his characters.

Alyona Ivanovna (alternately, Alëna): The old pawnbroker is not given a last name in the novel. Her profession puts her in a lower social class than Raskolnikov (despite the reality of their respective financial situations) so they would not likely use full names in addressing each other. She is an old woman, presented as a heartless crone who extorts usurious interest from those who pawn items with her. She devotes much of the money she makes in this manner to having prayers said for her soul.

Dementiev, Nikolai: He is alternately, and somewhat unusually, referred to as Mikolka, Mikolai or Nikolashka. No patronymic is given for him. A painter who was working in an apartment in Alyona Ivanovna's building at the time of the murder. He later confesses to the murders, thereby confounding Porfiry Petrovich's trap for Raskolnikov. Porfiry denies the validity of this confession, though, claiming that Dementiev only wishes to take on suffering as part of an unorthodox religious practice.

Lebezyatnikov, Andrei Semyonovich (alternately, Andrey): The verb *lebezit'* means "to flatter" or "to fawn over." Lebezyatnikov shares lodgings with Luzhin and embodies the progressive ideas of the time that Dostoyevsky disliked intensely. Lebezyatnikov initially does little in the novel except make overly grand, occasionally nonsensical, statements that vaguely resemble those of the Russian socialists. He gains some sympathy by exposing Pyotr Luzhin's false accusation of theft against Sonya Marmeladova.

Lippewechsel, Amalia Ivanovna: Her last name is of German origin, a nonsense phrase meaning something like "lip exchanging." Because of her German background, she is sometimes derisively given the decidedly un-Russian patronymic "Ludwigovna." She is more a caricature than a full character. She speaks broken and heavily accented Russian and constantly argues with Katerina Marmeladova. She evicts the Marmeladovs after the failed funeral dinner.

Lizaveta Ivanovna: Like her sister, Alyona Ivanovna, she is not given a last name either. Presented as a victim of Alyona's cruelty, she is a friend of Sonya Marmeladova, with whom she reads scripture. Raskolnikov murders her as well, although he had not planned to, because she comes into the apartment immediately after he has killed Alyona.

Luzhin, Pyotr Petrovich: His last name comes from the word for "puddle." A rich and very arrogant older man who is engaged to Avdotya Raskolnikova. He is presented throughout the novel as being very superficial and stingy. He and Rodion Raskolnikov do not get along at all. Luzhin tries to set Avdotya and her mother against Raskolnikov by slandering Sonya Marmeladova, with whom Raskolnikov has been associated. When Avdotya breaks off their engagement, he attempts one final means of discrediting Raskolnikov, contriving a plan through which he can accuse Sonya of having stolen some money from him. His plan is foiled, though, and he leaves in disgrace.

Marmeladova, Katerina Ivanovna: A widowed woman of noble birth who marries Semyon Marmeladov. She tries to have a proper funeral dinner for her second husband but the scene degenerates into an argument between herself and her landlady, Amalia Lippewechsel. She is evicted from her apartment, aggravates her already poor health and dies not long after.

Marmeladov, Semyon Zakharovich: His last name is derived from the Russian word for marmelade. He has lost several jobs because of his alcoholism. Sonya Marmeladova is his natural daughter and he has married Katerina Marmeladova, a widow with three younger children. He steals all the family's money, goes on a drinking spree and meets Rodion Raskolnikov. Marmeladov is later struck by a carriage in the street and dies soon afterward in his apartment, begging the forgiveness of his wife and daughter.

Marmeladova, Sofia Semyonovna (alternately, Sonya, Sonia, Sonechka, Sofya): Her name is derived from the Greek word for wisdom. Although eighteen years of age, she is still in many ways a child forced to act the part of an adult. Her father's drinking and theft force her to become a prostitute to make money for her family. She has a strong belief in God and righteous suffering and it is through her moral guidance that Rodion Raskolnikov achieves some sort of repentance by the end of the novel. She moves to Siberia when Raskolnikov is sent to prison there and becomes a spiritual inspiration for him because of her steadfast devotion.

Porfiry Petrovich: His last name is not given in the novel, perhaps because his investigation of Raskolnikov is never official, thus never making his relationship with Raskolnikov formal enough (by Russian standards) to warrant the use of his last name in address. He is the head detective of the precinct in which the murder of Alyona Ivanovna takes place. He suspects Rodion Raskolnikov of being the murderer and subtly pursues a course of inquiry designed to make Raskolnikov incriminate himself. He sets a trap for him that is spoiled by an unexpected false confession but later returns to Raskolnikov's room to directly accuse him of committing the murder.

Raskolnikov, Rodion Romanovich (alternately, Rodya, Rodenka, or Rodka): Dostoyevsky gave the protagonist of his novel a name that would have several associations for his readers. The name Raskolnikov is derived from the Russian word *raskol*, which means "schism." It is also similar to the name of the *Raskolniki*, a group of fundamentalist Russian Orthodox Christians who broke away from the Church in the seventeenth century over issues of religious practice. Like this group, Raskolnikov is a dissenter from the standard social order of his time. He is a young student who has been forced to drop out of school for financial reasons and has almost completely withdrawn from public life as the novel opens. He has published an article on his theory of the rights of a select few to transgress the law and, in part to test his theory, he decides to kill a wretched old pawnbroker, Alyona Ivanovna. By doing so, he hopes to discover whether he himself is among the select group. He kills the pawnbroker (and also her sister, although this is not planned) and then spends the remainder of the novel alternately calling himself into suspicion and trying not to get caught. He befriends an alcoholic clerk named Marmeladov and eventually assists his family after his accidental death. The oldest daughter, Sonya, especially draws his attention, and it is to her that he eventually confesses his crime for the first time. Raskolnikov undergoes a spiritual renewal in the epilogue of the novel after being sent to Siberia for his crimes.

Raskolnikova, Avdotya Romanovna (alternately, Dunya, Dounia, Dounya, Dounechka, or Dunechka): Rodion Raskolnikov's sister. She worked as a governess on the estate of Arkady Svidrigailov, but leaves after being falsely accused of immoral behavior. She is exonerated, though, and decides to marry Pyotr Luzhin, a rich nobleman, in order to help out her family's suffering finances. She angrily breaks off the engagement when Luzhin demonstrates his lack of interest in her well-being. She finds out about the murders that Raskolnikov has committed from Svidrigailov. She subsequently threatens Svidrigailov with a gun after he makes an unwanted offer not to disclose his knowledge of the crime if she will agree to become his mistress. She eventually marries Dmitri Razumikhin, who took care of Dunya and her mother after their arrival in St. Petersburg.

Raskolnikova, Pulcheria Alexandrovna (alternately, Pulkheria): Rodion Raskolnikov's mother. She is constantly worried about her son's state of affairs and moves to St. Petersburg along with her daughter, Avdotya. Pulcheria dies due to illness she contracts largely because of the emotional strain of Raskolnikov's trial.

Razumikhin, Dmitri Prokofich (alternately, Dmitry): His last name comes from the word *razum*, meaning "reason" or "intelligence." Rodion Raskolnikov's best friend and a fellow student. He oversees the care and recovery of Raskolnikov when he falls ill and offers to protect Avdotya Raskolnikova and her mother when they come to St. Petersburg. He introduces Raskolnikov to Porfiry Petrovich, unknowingly setting in motion the investigation that will lead to Raskolnikov's confession of the murder. After Raskolnikov's arrest and imprisonment, he marries Avdotya and resumes his studies at the university.

Svidrigailov, Arkady Ivanovich (alternately, Svidrigaylov): A rich, but unscrupulous landowner for whom Avdotya Raskolnikova worked as a governess. He married a considerably older woman, Marfa Svidrigailova, who bailed him out of debtor's prison. He makes a failed attempt to coerce Avdotya into having an affair with him, the result of which is Avdotya's erroneous banishment from the estate by an angry Marfa. He is haunted by visions of his wife after her death and moves to St. Petersburg to pursue Avdotya. He overhears Rodion Raskolnikov's confession of the murders to Sonya Marmeladova and tries to use this to blackmail Avdotya into submitting to his advances. However, she pulls a gun on him and he leaves in despair. After arranging for the financial care of Katerina Marmeladova's children with the last of his money, he kills himself.

Zamyotov, Aleksandr Grigorievich (alternately, Zametov): A young police clerk to whom Rodion Raskolnikov nearly confesses in a state of delirium.

Zarnitsyna, Praskovya Pavlovna (alternately, Pashenka): Raskolnikov's somewhat dimwitted landlady. Rodion Raskolnikov entertained notions of marrying her daughter, Natalia, but the girl died of typhus before this could happen.

PLOT SUMMARY

Part One As the novel opens, a somewhat downtrodden young student, Rodion Raskolnikov, is on his way to visit an old pawnbroker named Alyona Ivanovna. As he walks through the streets of St. Petersburg, he struggles with his conscience over a plan he has concocted to murder Ivanovna. Part of him is revolted by the thought of the crime, but he continues planning the hypothetical act anyway. After pawning a few items with the unpleasant and miserly Ivanovna, Raskolnikov stops off in a tavern.

Here, Raskolnikov meets Semyon Marmeladov, a drunkard who proceeds to tell him his sad life story. He tells Raskolnikov of how he previously lost his government job because of his drinking. Granted a reprieve, Marmeladov has resumed his work, but when Raskolnikov meets him, he has stolen money from his family to go on another lengthy drinking binge that will undoubtedly cost him his job again. Marmeladov is afraid to return home to his wife, Katerina Ivanovna. He tells Raskolnikov about his daughter, Sofia (nicknamed Sonya), and how she has become a prostitute in order to support the family.

Raskolnikov accompanies Marmeladov home, where he sees the poverty and violence in which his new acquaintance's family lives. Although almost destitute himself, Raskolnikov quietly leaves some money for the family. Immediately after doing so, though, he regrets his charity and wants to take the money back. This is the first instance in which the reader sees the internal conflict between Raskolnikov's sympathy for suffering and his intellectual rationalization of the scant good that his charity will do.

Raskolnikov returns to his cramped and dingy room. He is informed by his housekeeper that his landlady is planning to file a complaint with the police because Raskolnikov owes a great deal of rent. He also receives a long letter from his mother in which she describes the troubles that his sister, Avdotya (Dunya), has been experiencing. She had been working as a governess at the estate of a landowner named Arkady Svidrigailov. Svidrigailov unsuccessfully tried to seduce Dunya. Out of a mistaken belief that Dunya attempted to seduce her husband, Svidrigailov's wife, Marfa Petrovna, has been spreading slanderous gossip about Dunya. Once she learned the truth, though, Marfa tried to make amends, in part by convincing her distant relative Pyotr Petrovich Luzhin to propose marriage to Dunya.

Luzhin is a middle-aged aristocrat who desires a wife with a good reputation. However, he also wishes his wife to be somewhat impoverished so that she will be indebted to him. Raskolnikov's mother writes him that she and Dunya will be arriving in St. Petersburg shortly to finalize the plans for the marriage. Raskolnikov is infuriated at this news, believing that Dunya is marrying Luzhin out of a sense of martyrdom for the family's needs, especially his own.

Raskolnikov takes a walk to soothe his increasingly agitated mind. Somewhat lost in his own brooding thoughts, he notices a girl staggering down the street followed by a lecherous-looking man. Raskolnikov calls out for a policeman in order to protect the girl and even offers his last bit of money for a cab. Once again, he almost immediately regrets interfering in the situation, deciding that his emotions have become confused because of the news about his beloved sister and the story of Marmeladov's daughter. After this encounter, Raskolnikov decides to visit an old schoolmate, Dmitri Razumikhin, who had offered to provide him with some work doing translations.

Before he can get there, though, Raskolnikov decides he will delay his visit. He has a drink and falls asleep in the park, where he has a vivid and troubling dream that closely resembles an episode from Dostoyevsky's own childhood. Raskolnikov dreams that he is a young boy walking to his mother's grave alongside his father. While walking, they encounter a mass of drunken peasants, one of whom is trying to make an old horse pull an impossibly heavy wagon. The crowd ridicules this peasant, who in turn becomes enraged and begins brutally beating the horse, eventually killing it. The young Raskolnikov is so disturbed by this act that he runs over to the horse, flings his arms around its head and kisses it profusely.

Raskolnikov awakens and is even more profoundly disturbed. As he walks home, having made up his mind not to follow through on his plans for murder, he hears by chance that the old pawnbroker's sister, Lizaveta Ivanovna, will be out of the apartment on an errand between six and seven o'clock that evening. He goes into a tavern for a cup of tea and overhears a conversation between two young officers in which they discuss the relative merits of killing the old pawnbroker. They rationalize that getting rid of her would remove a wicked person from society and allow her vast amount of hoarded money to be used to assist destitute families. They also claim that the person who commits the murder would be serving humanity, thereby absolving himself of the crime.

Raskolnikov returns home and sleeps briefly before deciding that he will kill Alyona Ivanovna after all. His simultaneously meticulous and frenzied preparations are described in elaborate detail. However, he is so delayed by his preparations that he does not arrive at the old woman's apartment until seven-thirty. As Alyona Ivanovna cautiously opens her door to Raskolnikov, assuming he is bringing another item to pawn, he is almost delirious.

As she examines the item he has brought to distract her,

he commits the brutal murder by striking her twice with the blunt side of an axe. He finds her keys and hurriedly searches the room for money and other valuables. As he is doing so, he suddenly hears footsteps in the entryway and realizes that he has left the front door open. He returns to the living room to find Lizaveta standing there and splits her skull with his axe. Now in a state of panic, he tries to clean the blood from the axe and from himself. During this, the doorbell rings and Raskolnikov hides behind the door. The visitors realize that the door is locked from the inside and leave to get help. While they are gone, Raskolnikov slips out and hides in an empty flat on a lower floor. He returns home and falls almost immediately into a deep sleep.

Part Two When Raskolnikov awakens, he begins to be tormented both by his conscience and by the strategic mistakes he made in his planning and execution of the murder. He falls back into heavy, troubled sleep, only to be awakened by Nastasya, his landlady's servant, and a police officer knocking at his door. He is summoned to the police station and considers confessing his crime. When he arrives at the station, he learns that he is being questioned about the back rent he owes. While there, though, he hears several people talking about the murder of Alyona Ivanovna and faints. After recovering, he is even more concerned that the police suspect him and goes home to hide the things he took from Alyona Ivanovna's apartment.

Afterward, he goes to see Razumikhin, but he is unable to speak coherently with him. He starts for home and is almost run over by a coach. Back at home he falls into a feverish sleep. After several days, Raskolnikov recovers consciousness and finds that Razumikhin has been taking care of him, even going so far as to buy him some new clothes with money that Raskolnikov's mother has sent him.

Subsequently, Raskolnikov is visited by a doctor named Zosimov. The doctor and Razumikhin talk about the arrest of two painters in relation to the murders. This exchange excites Raskolnikov greatly, and Zosimov misinterprets his interest in the subject as a resumption of interest in life.

Luzhin comes to meet Raskolnikov while Zosimov is there. He is awkward and stiff in Raskolnikov's presence. Raskolnikov makes his dislike and distrust of Luzhin readily apparent; the two quarrel openly, with Raskolnikov angrily threatening bodily harm against Luzhin as he leaves.

Raskolnikov goes for another walk and ends up in a restaurant called the Crystal Palace, where he asks for the newspapers from the last five days. While reading the papers, he meets Zamyotov, a policeman and friend of Razumikhin. Raskolnikov dangerously begins to discuss the murder with Zamyotov, even going so far as to tell him how he would commit the crime. Zamyotov attributes Raskolnikov's odd behavior to his illness, seemingly letting him off the hook. However, Raskolnikov casts further suspicion on himself by returning to the scene of the crime and causing a commotion.

He resolves to turn himself in and is on his way to the police station when he sees Marmeladov, drunk, run over by a carriage. Raskolnikov arranges to have him taken home and accompanies the dying man back to the Marmeladovs' apartment. Marmeladov apologizes to his family but dies soon after. Raskolnikov gives Marmeladov's wife, Katerina Ivanovna, the money that his mother had sent him and then quickly leaves the scene. One of the Marmeladov children, Polenka, follows Raskolnikov to ask him his name and to thank him for his charity on behalf of her sister Sonya. Raskolnikov asks the girl to pray for him and departs. When he returns home he finds his mother and Dunya waiting for him.

Part Three Raskolnikov immediately states that he is opposed to Dunya's marriage, telling them of his confrontation with Luzhin. Razumikhin, still somewhat drunk from having earlier attended a party, offers his help to Dunya and her mother. He almost immediately develops a strong affection for Dunya. Razumikhin takes them back to their lodgings and then returns to Raskolnikov's room with Zosimov.

The doctor states that he is satisfied with Raskolnikov's progress, and Razumikhin relays this news to Dunya and her mother as well as details of Raskolnikov's life in the past year. In turn, Raskolnikov's mother, Pulcheria Ivanovna shows Razumikhin a letter from Luzhin requesting that Raskolnikov not be present at their first interview.

They apprehensively return to Raskolnikov's room, but Pulcheria is pleased to see that her son's condition is improved. However, Raskolnikov still insists that Dunya not marry Luzhin, even going so far as to say he will disown her as his sister if she goes through with the marriage. Dunya justifies the marriage to Raskolnikov, who grudgingly withdraws his objections. She shows him the letter from Luzhin but asks that he come anyway.

Sonya appears at Raskolnikov's apartment while Dunya and Pulcheria are there. She has come to invite him to Marmeladov's funeral and to the subsequent funeral meal. Sonya is embarrassed by the room's appearance, realizing that Raskolnikov must have given her family all his money. After an uncomfortable few moments in the room, she leaves. As Sonya walks home, she is followed by a strange man who turns out to live in the same house as she does. His name is Andrei Lebezyatnikov.

Raskolnikov tells Razumikhin that he wants an interview with Porfiry Petrovich, the chief detective of the police and a cousin to Razumikhin. Upon meeting with Porfiry Petrovich, Raskolnikov tells him that he had pawned some items with Alyona Ivanovna that he wanted to get back, supposedly for sentimental value. Porfiry Petrovich lets on that he already knows some details of Raskolnikov's life (thus making him a suspect in the case) and also asks him to explain parts of an article that he wrote on the nature of crime. Raskolnikov's article concerns a theory by which certain extraordinary individuals can be absolved from responsibility for transgressions of the law because their actions are eventually designed for a greater good. Raskolnikov even goes so far as to claim that such murderers are justified, ranking them among the likes of Napoléon and Mohammed. Porfiry Petrovich asks Raskolnikov if he thinks of himself as an extraordinary man. He also tries to trip Raskolnikov up by asking if he remembers seeing any painters on the day he went to pawn his things with Alyona Ivanovna. Raskolnikov evades the traps, though, and Razumikhin becomes indignant that Porfiry Petrovich would even consider Raskolnikov a suspect.

Raskolnikov returns to his room and searches his memory for any clues he may have left behind at the crime scene. Having reassured himself that he did not, he sets off to meet his mother and sister. When Raskolnikov begins trembling and becomes frightened, he returns to his room and falls asleep. He dreams that he is again striking the old woman but she refuses to die. When he awakens, he sees a man standing in the doorway who introduces himself as Arkady Svidrigailov, Dunya's former employer.

Part Four Svidrigailov tells Raskolnikov his life story—one that is in many ways similar to Raskolnikov's. He describes the death of his wife, Marfa Petrovna, and how she has appeared to him in ghostly form since her death. He makes an offer to pay Dunya ten thousand rubles not to marry Luzhin.

After this, Raskolnikov and Razumikhin meet with Dunya, Pulcheria Ivanovna, and Luzhin. The meeting goes badly, and Luzhin quickly demonstrates that he is self-absorbed and conniving. Furthermore, Luzhin tries to estrange Raskolnikov from his family by implying that his relationship with Sonya has been improper and immoral. Dunya is highly offended by Luzhin's behavior and breaks off their engagement. Luzhin makes a final insolent remark, at which Razumikhin flies into a rage and is restrained from physically assaulting Luzhin in defense of Dunya.

Raskolnikov leaves Razumikhin to care for his sister and mother and goes to Sonya's apartment. They talk about the fate that is in store for her family, and Sonya insists that God will take care of them. Raskolnikov mocks her religious faith. He makes her read the story of Lazarus to him, ironically from a Bible given to her by Lizaveta Ivanovna. After this, he tells her that he is leaving his family and has only her left in his life. Raskolnikov tells her that he knows who killed Lizaveta and that he will tell her the next day. Unbeknownst to either of them, Svidrigailov is listening through the door of the adjoining room.

The next day, Raskolnikov goes to see Porfiry Petrovich in his office to make a claim for the items he had pawned. Porfiry Petrovich treats him very amicably, much to Raskolnikov's confusion, and talks to him more about the article that Raskolnikov had written and about his theories on the murder of Alyona Ivanovna. Raskolnikov is convinced that Porfiry Petrovich is about to accuse him of the murder and begins to angrily defend himself, even as Porfiry Petrovich denies any accusation. The tension finally breaks when Nikolai Dementiev, one of the painters from Alyona Ivanovna's building, bursts in and unexpectedly confesses to the murders. Porfiry Petrovich is skeptical, but he has no choice and must allow Raskolnikov to leave. Raskolnikov hurries to the Marmeladovs' apartment for Semyon Marmeladov's funeral dinner.

Part Five As this section opens, Luzhin is talking with Andrei Lebezyatnikov. Their conversation reveals both of them to be shallow and superficial, even perhaps somewhat evil. Luzhin prepares a trap for Sonya, which he will spring later at the dinner. He intends to prove to Dunya that her brother's companion is immoral by framing Sonya for theft. He gives her ten rubles, ostensibly to help out with the family's needs, while at the same time surreptitiously slipping another hundred-ruble bill in the pocket of her dress. However, Lebezyatnikov sees this from the other room.

The banquet itself is tragicomic. Katerina Ivanovna, seriously ill with consumption, invites everyone from the apartment building to the dinner, but the guests who arrive are a rogue's gallery. Raskolnikov arrives, much to Katerina Ivanovna's delight, but her happiness soon turns to anger as she gets into a heated argument with her German landlady, Amalia Lippewechsel.

Luzhin enters the room and accuses Sonya of having ungratefully stolen money from him while he tried to do a good deed for her family. He dramatically produces the hundred rubles from her pocket, and Sonya breaks down into tears. Lebezyatnikov, however, does not allow Luzhin to get away with his treachery and tells the gathered company that he saw Luzhin plant the bill on Sonya. Luzhin leaves in disgrace and is narrowly missed by a thrown glass as he exits the door. This glass hits Amalia Ivanovna, though, and she responds by forcibly evicting the Marmeladovs from the building.

Raskolnikov goes with Sonya to her apartment and tearfully confesses his crimes to her. She is initially horrified but begs him to turn himself in and to accept his punishment. She also promises to follow him to Siberia. Raskolnikov says that he is not yet ready to accept his punishment and leaves just as Lebezyatnikov arrives.

Lebezyatnikov informs Sonya that Katerina Ivanovna has gone mad. They all leave, and Raskolnikov returns to his apartment as the others go to look for Katerina. Dunya comes to see Raskolnikov, but he bids her farewell, telling her that Razumikhin is a good man. Lebezyatnikov finds Raskolnikov on the street and tells him of Katerina's frenzied wanderings through the streets; and they return to Sonya's apartment just as Katerina is dying. Svidrigailov appears and offers to pay for the funeral and to take care of the children. He also implies that he knows that Raskolnikov is the murderer, having overheard his confession to Sonya from his room.

Part Six Razumikhin comes to see Raskolnikov, and Raskolnikov tells him that he wishes him to take care of Dunya and his mother. Razumikhin leaves, believing that

Raskolnikov is involved in some political intrigue. Porfiry Petrovich also visits Raskolnikov and tells him his theories about why Nikolai Dementiev could not be the murderer. He does not accuse Raskolnikov directly, but he tells Raskolnikov that he wants him to confess of his own free will. He also tells Raskolnikov that he is not afraid of his fleeing.

Raskolnikov hurriedly leaves his apartment in search of Svidrigailov, eventually finding him in a tavern. He threatens Svidrigailov, telling him not to see Dunya. Svidrigailov calms Raskolnikov somewhat and talks to him about his feelings for Dunya, trying to justify his attraction to her and demonstrate the flaws in his own nature.

Raskolnikov follows Svidrigailov after they leave the tavern, but Svidrigailov taunts him with his knowledge of the murder, and they part company after a short while. Svidrigailov meets Dunya in the street. He tempts her to his apartment, where he tells her that her brother murdered the pawnbroker and Lizaveta Ivanovna. He tries to blackmail her with this information, offering his silence for her love. She refuses and pulls a gun on him. She tries to shoot him twice but fails. Svidrigailov embraces her, but she rejects him once more. He dejectedly tells her that she can leave, and she does just that.

Svidrigailov goes out and spends the evening in a number of taverns. After this he goes to Sonya and gives her the money he had mentioned to Raskolnikov. He leaves Sonya and takes a room for a night in a hotel. Here, he has an odd dream and ends up committing suicide the next morning with the remaining bullet from Dunya's gun.

Raskolnikov visits his mother and sister. He asks his mother to pray for him and has a long conversation with Dunya about the nature and meaning of suffering. He leaves for Sonya's apartment, where he asks her to give him a cross that he had refused earlier. He tells her that he will make a confession, not to Porfiry Petrovich, but at a public crossroads in St. Petersburg. Sonya follows him out to the crossroads, but he changes his mind after being mistaken for a drunkard when he falls to his knees. He then decides to go to the police station. There, he learns of Svidrigailov's suicide and subsequently confesses to Zamyotov.

Epilogue The epilogue tells the story of Raskolnikov's trial and exile. He is sentenced to eight years in Siberia, and Sonya follows him into exile. Raskolnikov's mother had fallen ill because of the stress associated with her son's trial, and dies shortly after he leaves for Siberia. Razumikhin marries Dunya two months after Raskolnikov's exile. In the beginning of his imprisonment, Raskolnikov is still somewhat unrepentant, but he gradually finds the means to change his ways through Sonya's example. She ministers both to him and to many of the other prisoners. When she falls ill, Raskolnikov finally realizes how much she (and the faith she represents) means to him, and he begins the process of his gradual renewal.

CHAPTER 1

The Critical Reception of *Crime and Punishment*

READINGS ON
CRIME AND PUNISHMENT

Why You Should Read "A Terrible Novel"

Lafcadio Hearn

Lafcadio Hearn (1850–1903) was a trailblazer in American literary criticism. In addition to being one of the first white scholars to take African American literature seriously, he also wrote extensively on Oriental and other foreign authors, including Dostoyevsky. In this brief review, published in 1885 in a New Orleans newspaper, Hearn argues that *Crime and Punishment* is an extraordinary work despite the fact that it is, in his words, a "terrible novel" in the traditional sense. Hearn claims that the book's importance lies not in its plot or its verbal style (elements traditionally held in high regard in novels), but in its powerful ability to depict the human psyche. In making this distinction, Hearn became one of the first American critics to value the less explicit elements of artistic creation that marked Dostoyevsky's fiction.

In Paris, Russian literature continues to be the sensation. The *Nouvelle Revue* in its latest issue, gives an admirable summary of the history of the elder and of the new schools of that literature, with condensed notices of Gogol; Tourgueneff; Tutcheff, the poet; Ostrowsky, the pupil of Gogol; Gribojedoff, the Russian comedy-writer; Leon and Alexis Tolstoi; Pissemsky; Joukowsky, tutor of Alexander II; Kriloff, the Russian La Fontaine; Boleslas Markevitch, the student whose novels treat of modern Nihilism, and who dared even to make the assassination of the late Emperor the subject of a superb romance. Meanwhile three or four Paris publishers are turning out monthly new translations of the masterpieces of Gogol, Pouchkine, and many others, or printing new editions of translations which had appeared at a less favorable era only to be forgotten. Among these sensations are

Reprinted from Lafcadio Hearn, "A Terrible Novel," *New Orleans Times Democrat*, November 22, 1885, as it appeared in *Essays in European and Oriental Literature*, edited by Albert Mordell (New York: Dodd & Mead, 1923).

the works of Leon Tolstoi—enormous novels which require weeks to read;—reproductions of Mérimée's translations of Russian dramas and novelettes; the latest volumes of Tourgueneff; and two notable works by Dostoievsky, the Siberian exile. One of these last forms, perhaps, the most frightful and powerful romance conceived by any modern writer. Appearing in 1866, it made a sensation in Russia far more profound than that created first in France by the work of Jean Jacques Rousseau. It gave the nightmare to the entire reading population of the empire. Many who read it became seriously ill in consequence. A still greater number could not summon courage to finish it; for the horror of the narration,—incessantly augmented through all the pages of two great volumes, as the horror of a sick dream continually increases with its protraction,—so unnerved them that they hid the romance away and dared not look at it again. These statements may seem exaggerations to American readers, or to European readers, who imagine that they have become familiar with all possibilities of plot and all artifices of literary style. Nevertheless there is only the thinnest possible plot in this terrible novel, and no artifices of style whatever. The power of the work is not in workmanship of phrases, or ingenuity of conception;—it is a psychical force,—a sort of ghastly mesmerism like that exercised by Coleridge's fantastic mariner. And the story is not a supernatural one; it deals only with possibilities and realisms;—but the possibilities are the extremes of suffering that a human mind may endure, and the realisms are pictures of a soul in living agony. Any intelligent person who has tried to read the book will probably confirm all that has been said regarding its power of terrorism. Nothing exists in print so horribly fascinating and yet so frightfully repellent as Dostoievsky's *Crime and Punishment*.

Theodore Dostoievsky, born in 1822, entered upon his literary career at a time when the social paroxysms of Russia had inaugurated what has since been well-termed The Dynamic Period. The era of violence had not reached its greatest intensity when he began to enter upon manhood; but before he died, in 1880, he had passed through the worst of it. He left the army, for which he was educated, to devote himself to literary work; and became a writer of mark at the very epoch when the profession of author was most difficult, most dangerous, and most underpaid. Already the careers of Russian authors had been, as a rule, peculiarly sinister.

Pouchkine and Lermontof were both killed in duels; Ryllief was executed as a revolutionary; Polejaief, Bestulssev and Baraktinski died in exile; Venjevitenof and Kolizof died of starvation; Batjushkof and Gogol went mad. Others had equally dismal destinies. The Russian soul, struggling for utterance, under a mountain weight of oppression, was everywhere manifesting symptoms strangely akin to madness. Mysticism, reverie, hopeless ambition, vain rage mark the psychology of the time. Dostoievsky himself was menaced with insanity. He was saved from it only by a more active life; but that life led him to Siberia. He returned, a wiser man, but not a sadder one—(for the world has known no sadder soul than his)—to write his awful book.

The plot is simple indeed. An educated sensitive student, struggling with the world for bread, and filled with the dangerous philosophy of his time, conceives that to murder a wicked person, to take away the wealth of that person, and use it for a good purpose, are not essentially evil actions. To him the world contains but two classes of people,—the Extraordinary and the Ordinary. The Extraordinary are privileged to do as they please by mere virtue of the fact that they are Extraordinary;—the Ordinary people only are created to obey laws,—to be good fathers and mothers, and industrious citizens. Imagining himself Extraordinary the student begins life by murdering a rich old hag and her sister in order "to devote their wealth to the good of his fellow-creatures." Then he finds out he is only Ordinary! His nerves give way; his physical and reasoning powers prove inferior to his will. After years of hideous mental struggles he is compelled to denounce himself to the police as the assassin. Yet he does not imagine himself morally guilty; his mental sufferings are not the sufferings of remorse, but of nervous affection. He speaks only in order to save himself from going mad. If he ever comprehends his crime, it is in the solitude of his Siberian prison, and through the moral teaching of a poor fallen woman who loves him.

A very thin plot apparently; but the details fill two volumes (nearly 700 pages!) in all of which there is not one dull line. The power of the book lies in its marvelous dissection of intricate mental characteristics,—in its unaffected intensity of realism,—in a verisimilitude so extraordinary that the reader is compelled to believe himself the criminal, to feel the fascination of the crime, to endure the excitement of it, to enjoy the perpetration of it, to vibrate with the terror of it, to suffer all the nightmares, all the horrors, all the degradation, all the punishment of it. This is what causes so terrible a nervous strain upon the reader. He actually *becomes* Raskol-

THE RIME OF THE ANCIENT MARINER

Hearn compares the effect of reading Crime and Punishment *to that of the audience hearing the story of the sailor who killed an albatross in Samuel Taylor Coleridge's poem, "The Rime of the Ancient Mariner." Compare some of this excerpt from the poem (taken from the section immediately following the mariner's "inhospitable" killing of the bird) to Dostoyevsky's descriptions of Raskolnikov after the murder of Alyona Ivanovna.*

The Sun now rose upon the right:
Out of the sea came he,
Still hid in mist, and on the left
Went down into the sea.

And the good south wind still blew behind,
But no sweet bird did follow,
Nor any day for food or play
Came to the mariners' hollo!

And I had done an hellish thing,
And it would work 'em woe:
For all averred, I had killed the bird
That made the breeze to blow.

Ah wretch! said they, the bird to slay,
That made the breeze to blow!
Nor dim nor red, like God's own head,
The glorious Sun uprist:

Then all averred, I had killed the bird
That brought the fog and mist.
'Twas right, said they, such birds to slay,
That bring the fog and mist.

The fair breeze blew, the white foam flew,
The furrow followed free;
We were the first that ever burst
Into that silent sea.

Down dropt the breeze, the sails dropt down,
'Twas sad as sad could be;
And we did speak only to break
The silence of the sea!

nikoff the murderer, and feels, thinks, dreams, trembles as the criminal whose psychology is thus exposed for him! The perusal of the pages seems to produce a sort of avatar, a change of souls; if the reader is not wholly Raskolnikoff, he

All in a hot and copper sky,
The bloody Sun, at noon,
Right up above the mast did stand,
No bigger than the Moon.

Day after day, day after day,
We stuck, nor breath nor motion;
As idle as a painted ship
Upon a painted ocean.

Water, water, every where,
And all the boards did shrink;
Water, water, every where,
Nor any drop to drink.

The very deep did rot: O Christ!
That ever this should be!
Yea, slimy things did crawl with legs
Upon the slimy sea.

About, about, in reel and rout
The death-fires danced at night;
The water, like a witch's oils,
Burnt green, and blue and white.

And some in dreams assuréd were
Of the Spirit that plagued us so;
Nine fathom deep he had followed us
From the land of mist and snow.

And every tongue, through utter drought,
Was withered at the root;
We could not speak, no more than if
We had been choked with soot.

Ah! well a-day! what evil looks
Had I from old and young!
Instead of the cross, the Albatross
About my neck was hung.

Excerpted from Samuel Taylor Coleridge, "The Rime of the Ancient Mariner" in the *Norton Anthology of English Literature.*

is at least wholly Dostoievsky the author, nearly crazed by his own thoughts. And all the personages of the narrative live with the same violence of realism. Gogol was Dostoievsky's teacher; but never did he write so puissant a book as this.

No book, moreover, has ever given so singular a revelation to French criticism. Here is an author, who, without attempt at style, without effort at form, without refinement of utterance, creates a book in open violation of all esthetic canons, and more powerful than any fiction written in strict obedience to them. A similar phenomenon,—though less pronounced perhaps,—may be discerned in most Russian writers, not excepting the most artistic of all, Tourgueneff. What is the secret of this immense superiority of the semi-barbaric Russian novel? Is it that the life of other civilizations, while more complex and refined, is also more factitious; and that Russian thought—Antaeus-like,—owes its power to a closer contact with mighty nature than our artificial existence allows of?

The Russian Perspective— 100 Years Later

Daniil Granin

As part of the foreword to a 1985 English-language edition of *Crime and Punishment* in the Soviet Union, the editors reprinted an article by Daniil Granin, a noted Russian intellectual and writer of fiction. In it, Granin discusses the one-hundredth anniversary of Dostoyevsky's death and the place he still occupies in Russian literature. Granin argues that Dostoyevsky's chief contribution to Russian (and world) literature was his depiction of human psychology, a subject that has become more common in modern fiction and in critical interpretation of literature in general.

The centenary of the death of Fyodor Dostoyevsky was observed throughout the world on February 8, 1981; the eyes of people in many lands, at universities in Czechoslovakia and Australia, Britain and Japan, the U.S. and Sweden were turned towards the three-storey house in a St. Petersburg side-street where the writer lay dying on that far-off winter day. Throughout the years he spent in the then Russian capital, his attention was held by the slum districts that housed poorer students and petty civil servants, the squalid furnished rooms, sunless courtyards, littered market-places and low taverns.

Despite the long and chequered path travelled by mankind during the past hundred years, Dostoyevsky's novels and stories have lost nothing of their lustre; indeed, they have gained a new stature, a new and sometimes strange cogency, revealing something like prevision in its way. They contain many passages, especially in *The Possessed* or *The Karamazov Brothers,* that are too prescient for them to be considered merely fortuitous surmises. It would seem that

Reprinted, with permission, from "On Fyodor Dostoyevsky (1821–81)," by Daniil Granin, *Novy Mir,* no. 3, 1981, as it appeared in the Foreword to *Crime and Punishment* (Moscow: Raduga, 1985), translated by Julius Katzer.

his genius gave him a presentiment of the road awaiting mankind, a kind of divination. Perhaps it is such stuff that genius is made on!

I once had occasion to be taken by Andrei Dostoyevsky, the writer's grandson, on a kind of conducted tour of Dostoyevsky's St. Petersburg, places associated with *Crime and Punishment.* It was a revealing experience: the places now all acquired authenticity; they were all there to see—it was here that Dostoyevsky lived, and there the Marmeladovs.

Many writers have indicated the exact addresses, the topography of the places the action in their stories is set: Pushkin did so with the Mikhailovsky estate, Dickens with his London, and [Ivan] Bunin with his Yelnia. Landscapes and urban locations are part and parcel of the narrative, are woven into its fabric, forming a kind of backdrop. Not so with Dostoyevsky: he has eyes only for what bears directly on the drama. At Raskolnikov's side, he counts the number of paces from the ex-student's house to the old usuress's flat in the house he, the author, has chosen for the purpose; he accompanies the murderer-to-be into the entrance, up the stairs, and right to her door. Dostoyevsky is, as it were, enacting the drama as playwright and stage director. He has to see the unfolding of the tragedy, and understand how it all comes about. Though Raskolnikov is his own creation, Dostoyevsky wants to understand him to the very end. In many ways, Raskolnikov is a mystery to him, but he wants to understand him and, to do so, brings forward a number of versions. He has no grounds for pretence because he knows so much: Raskolnikov's thoughts, feelings, words and actions, but that is not enough to establish the young man's motives, the pre-conscious urges that drive Raskolnikov, in the teeth of all logic. All this is puzzling Dostoyevsky, who sees so many of his characters as mysteries. Myshkin [in *The Idiot*] is a mystery, and so are Ivan Karamazov and Stavrogin [in *The Devils*].

DOSTOYEVSKY'S UNIQUE PLACE IN LITERATURE

Leo Tolstoy helps us to understand man; he shows us the impulses in his nature, the sources his thoughts spring from. He guides us into the depths of his soul.

Dostoyevsky helps us to grasp the impossibility of ever knowing man; he shows us how unfathomable man is, how chaotic his feelings, and how much there is in him that is contradictory and beyond understanding.

Therein lies much of the tribute of respect for man on Dostoyevsky's part. This is a lesson to writers. What is our showing in this regard? We know too much about the people that inhabit our stories; they are quite transparent to us; they are more familiar to us than our own kith and kin. We know everything about them, even the least circumstance. We analyse our characters down to the minutest trait.

That is, in some measure, a reflection of our times, the epoch of the scientific and technological revolution, in which our behaviour is quite pragmatic and subordinated to the logic of circumstances, to the advantage of some matter in hand. People of this type are necessary, I suppose. They are convenient and in keeping with a something: if that is so, then Dostoyevsky provides some protection from such a man-as-advantage, man-as-a-function. He comes out in defence of the mystery in man, his supreme destiny.

To Dostoyevsky, psychology is an instrument for an exploration of life's main problems, that of faith probably standing in the foreground. What is man to believe in? Does God exist? It would be naive to suppose that atheism can cancel the problem of man's faith, his faith in harmony, in universal happiness, and man's special destiny.

If one would speak of the lessons Dostoyevsky can teach our times, then one should realise that the range of the problems he raised are not mere particulars of boldly presented questions concerning events under way, even though he lived, suffered, and felt so deeply involved in political and other matters of public concern at the time. No, the issues he raised were of a burning topicality, yet eternal at the same time. It is most instructive how, in his stories, sheer topicality became transmuted and sublimed, giving rise, not to abstract propositions but to throbbing ideas bathed in tears and blood.

He fearlessly showed the fate awaiting those who were without faith: it had forsaken them; the gods had gone, died. He was tormented by the question: what awaits mankind if there is no God? What will come about if the god in man yields place to some powerful personality to whom anything is permissible? In that case, what will be when all that is human in man disappears, is destroyed? How is that to be stood up to? What is man entitled to? Has any man the right to dispose of another's life so as to benefit yet others? Who was the murderer of Fyodor Karamazov? How is the battle between good and evil progressing in man's soul? Does immortality exist? Whence the duality in man, his double nature? Dostoyevsky probed one by one into the problems of existence, of suffering, evil, love, crime, madness, passion, and greed.

DOSTOYEVSKY DEPICTS HUMAN NATURE

Philosophical cogency is a feature of his artistic genius: he is constantly engrossed in radical and decisive questions. To him, literature is a mode of thought: the writer is noteworthy, not so much for his skill in observing life's details, its colours, smells, catchwords, and particulars as for the agonising work of his thinking, which grapples with questions of the meaning of life. Therein lies Dostoyevsky's power, the example he sets to literature today.

There is nothing pedestrian about his writings, for he was able to discern the fantastic in Russian life.

Though the action may be laid in some actually existing city, everything there is fantastic. There is no awesome devilry here: reality is given a slight shift of focus, imperceptible at times, this giving a glimpse into gorges and chasms whose existence one has never even suspected.

Dostoyevsky makes difficult and at times unpleasant reading. Why is that? One does not come across anything naturalistic or any relish for scenes of violence and horror in his stories. This is a complex question I am not prepared to answer, but I would like to draw attention to a characteristic of his genius: it lays human imperfection bare. Thus: ". . . the usual human sense of pleasure at the sight of another's misfortune, that is to say, at seeing another break a leg, forfeit his honour, lose a loved creature, or the like . . ." (*The Hobbledehoy*); ". . . the lodgers began to press back towards the door, with that strange inner sense of satisfaction which is always to be seen even among the next of kin whenever disaster strikes our neighbour, and from which not one of us, without exception, is immune, however sincere our pity and commiseration" (from the scene of Marmeladov's death in *Crime and Punishment*.)

Of course, no one is willing to unearth such things within himself, yet, in some mysterious fashion, Dostoyevsky makes one discover within one's soul whatever is reprehensible there, those very passions that torment his characters. We become accomplices and are at fault, as it were; we have been unmasked and exposed. It appears that we are no better than they are, and are prepared to act in just the same way. When we read, in *The Hobbledehoy*, of man's ability to nurture the highest ideals in his breast, this cheek by jowl with the basest malice—and all that quite sincerely—does that belong only in people of the past?

WHAT READING DOSTOYEVSKY CAN DO FOR A MODERN AUDIENCE

The way Dostoyevsky is read and his books are *overcome* is, in some measure, a criterion of a society's moral aspirations.

Reading Dostoyevsky evokes a sense of shame in us—surely a precious property of his genius, which should teach us a lesson, if that is something that can be learnt. It puts us to shame and arouses our conscience, and that is why he is so hard to read. He disconcerts us and exorcises all attempts at evasion, any justification of the immoral and the evil. And how powerful is his branding of meanness, hypocrisy, sanctimoniousness, and cruelty! No, his is no morbid talent, but rather a cleansing one; it is humane, not cruel. Perhaps, when we set out to depict only that which is good, kindly, noble, and virtuous, and when we pick out and laud what is fine and exemplary, we are merely lulling our consciences, lowering our moral standards, and flattering people. The prestige achieved by our literature has, in particular, been enhanced by its indefatigable exposure of delusions and vice. That redounds to the credit, not only of Dostoyevsky but also of Russia's great literature which has always had the courage to speak words of wrath and sorrow to its people.

It is not easy to stir the conscience of present-day man, for it is subtly and firmly protected by a kind of carapace. Yet, like no one else, Dostoyevsky has been able to arouse that conscience, this making him belong to our day and age.

He stimulates thought: the world's most outstanding thinkers, psychologists, and scientists have felt and acknowledged his influence. Dostoyevsky studies have produced a remarkable literature of philosophical and scientific value, unique in its own right.

It is only the artist, the writer in the first place, that can help people discover new truths about themselves. In this sense, Dostoyevsky is the pride of Russia and her literature, indeed of world literature, and the long history of art.

I do not know what leads up to books being written. "Poetry is the purpose of poetry," as Pushkin once said. What is the prime cause here? What is the driving force in the artist, the purpose of his efforts? Is it enjoyment, edification, or scientific curiosity? I do not know. Yet all these are to be found in Dostoyevsky's writings in the highest degree. Moreover, they convey a sense of something miraculous, which keeps on attracting both our feelings and our minds, elevating them, and enabling us to see ourselves and the world of man in all its transience and its grandeur, its virtues and its values—all our world, its beauty and the inscrutability of its existence.

A Leftist View of *Crime and Punishment*

Alfred Kazin

Alfred Kazin, perhaps one of the best-known American social and literary critics of the twentieth century, wrote the introduction to a 1947 edition of *Crime and Punishment*. Its publication represented the first reprint of the novel since World War II, and thus the first reprint of what would soon be called the cold war era. Kazin was notably and consistently associated with liberal politics during his lifetime (although he was also notable for his criticism of Marxism—something of a rarity among American liberal intellectuals of his generation). Kazin's introduction to the book tells as much about how Dostoyevsky's ideas were a part of Russia in the late nineteenth century as it does about what lessons the book holds for the increasingly complex postwar world. As you read, keep the events surrounding the time of its writing clearly in mind.

Crime and Punishment is not only one of the great novels of the world; it is one of the most familiar—so familiar that probably everyone is sure he has read it. But it is a book whose original intention is often forgotten, for Dostoevsky was so great a narrator that his story eclipsed its "moral." He wrote it as a melodrama, but one that had a lesson or warning in it. For him it was a parable of the fate of nihilistic and sceptical youth in nineteenth-century Russia, whose materialism and revolutionary opinions he hated and feared. His book was to be a vision of the ultimate error and moral suffering of those who had so cut themselves off from established authority and morality that they had lost all respect for human life. To scare his readers into realizing how far such men could go, he had his youthful hero commit a mur-

Introduction, by Alfred Kazin, Copyright ©1946 by Alfred Kazin, to *Crime and Punishment*, by Fedor Dostoevsky, translated by Constance Garnett (Cleveland: World, 1946). Reprinted with the permission of The Wylie Agency, Inc.

der. Ever since, the world has read the book as one of the great thrillers, and let the moral go.

Crime and Punishment is a murder story, one of the greatest; it is a detective story, and there is probably little in detective fiction that rivals the psychological duel between the murderer and the police inspector, Porfiry. Yet it is a murder story like no other in the world, for the murder is not really important to the book; and the relation between murderer and detective is not between opponents, but between an erring son and a mocking father. The murder is only a stage background, and Porfiry is only another of Raskolnikov's friends and relations who are powerless to help him. The real subject of the book is the mind of Raskolnikov, and the real story takes place in his mind.

"Raskolnikov" is not really a man's proper name; it is, I am told, a play on the Russian word for "schismatic," someone who has cut himself off from the main body. To Dostoevsky, who by 1866, when he published the novel, had so lived down his own liberal youth that he had become one of the most vociferous defenders of Church and State, the novel was to be the story of a rebel, an outsider; of a lonely student who in his misery entertained delusions of power, and sought to prove his independence of morality by committing a murder. Raskolnikov had become for Dostoevsky the great symbol of the futility, the barrenness, the inevitable wickedness, of a sceptical intelligentsia.

Yet if this had been all, *Crime and Punishment* would have been only a dreary and even vicious satire on what was best in nineteenth-century Russian life—in that world of misery which it took the cataclysmic Russian revolution to uproot, and in which, as one Russian statesman confessed, "there are only beggars and philosophers." Raskolnikov belongs with the philosophers, not with the criminals. He is a freethinker in every sense of the word, and it is just the freedom of his thought that Dostoevsky fears. Yet we have here a book of such fantastic and immediate insight into a mind torn by conflict that we feel in reading it that we have been plunged to the depths, the forgotten and seemingly indescribable depths, of the human mind's war against itself. Why is this? Why did Dostoevsky begin with so moralistic, even so political (and what politics!) an intention, and create one of the universal symbols of the mind in crisis? It is because Dostoevsky hates Raskolnikov's philosophy, but loves Raskolnikov. Raskolnikov is his Hamlet, his deranged prince—a prince passing through great turmoil, unkind to those who love him best, suspicious of everyone; a prince who has killed, as Hamlet killed Polonius, out of impatience at his own weakness—yet a prince nevertheless, one of the true souls among men. Dostoevsky abominates the murder, but the murder is only a symbol of the error which a purely intellectual conception of life creates; he loves the murderer. In fact, he is himself Raskolnikov.

DOSTOEVSKY AS POLITICAL OUTSIDER

Dostoevsky always remained an outsider himself, though he tried to leap on the bandwagon of Russian orthodoxy and conformism. He felt his own alienation so deeply that he tried to suppress it by mocking the revolutionaries, the thoughtful young men of old Russia. But he never succeeded. He always remained with those he had condemned, for he was all his life one of the condemned. Nowhere is this better revealed than in the immediate human scene of this novel—the dank summer of St. Petersburg, the Hay Market, the horrible rattrap rooms, the pot-houses, the misery of the Marmeladov family, the world he so easily recreated of the poor, the sick, the criminal, the failures. Contrast the gravity and tenderness with which he writes of his hero, of the young prostitute Sonia, of Razumihin (Horatio to Raskolnikov's Hamlet), with the loathing he feels for Luzhin, the phony opportunist who always plays everything safe. Dostoevsky gave himself always to those who stood outside respectable society. He always remained one of the great outcasts himself.

Like Raskolnikov, Dostoevsky had stood outside the law and been condemned to Siberia. His own life was such a succession of storms that nothing so clearly reveals the supreme quality of his genius as the fact that his great novels were written under conditions that would have paralyzed anyone else. His father was an army doctor, and the boy was brought up in an atmosphere of army routine and petty politics, clinics, and savage parental tyranny. The father was so vicious and parsimonious that he seems to have treated his serfs and his children in the same fashion. The serfs, at least, openly revolted, and the father was murdered by them on his country estate. [Sigmund] Freud, who venerated Dostoevsky's genius, once wrote a brilliant essay to show that Dostoevsky had so longed to kill the father that he took on a burden of imaginary guilt after the murder occurred. However this was, there is no doubt that Dostoevsky's life-long obsession with murder had its roots in this traumatic experience of childhood. As a young army cadet he planned to become an engineer, but his literary interests drew him into the circles of the liberal student intelligentsia of the time. It was a period of bitter reaction in Russia, for Nicholas I was so alarmed by the rising tide of dissent that men were executed for "dangerous thoughts." Dostoevsky's own friends composed a mildly liberal group; most of its members were guilty of no greater "crime" than reading the utopian socialists. But they were arrested, and several of them, with Dostoevsky, were sentenced to death. At the last minute, when they were blindfolded and awaiting execution, they were suddenly "pardoned." The grisly mock-execution had been carefully arranged from the first, to frighten them.

Dostoevsky was sentenced to labor as a convict in the salt-mines of Siberia; afterwards he served as a common soldier in the ranks, and only with the greatest difficulty was able to return to Russia and recover his civil rights. Until his death in 1881, he lived the precarious life of a free-lance writer and wrote his books under the burden of debt, poverty, and illness. He was subject to frequent epileptic fits; his first marriage was a complete failure; all his efforts to found magazines fell under the mountain of debt he always incurred. His greatest novels were written at newspaper speed, for shrewd magazine editors who usually took advantage of his financial desperation to get his work at the lowest prices, and in the shortest possible time. He was so dependent on publishers that he once signed a contract agreeing to forfeit all rights to his next two books if the novel he was then working on was not completed within the stipulated period!

The effect of his early disgrace and constant suffering was to transform Dostoevsky into a fanatical exponent of authority. He had paid so dearly for his own small flight into liberalism, and by his own inner conflicts was prey to so much personal strife, that he forced himself to regard the ruling powers of Russia as the only safeguard. Religion, authority, and nationalism became a kind of parental world in which he could harbor himself, in which he could destroy the memory of his real or imaginary transgressions. On the surface he became one of the leaders of reactionary thought in

Russia, and certainly the only great Russian writer of the time who attacked the liberals and revolutionaries rather than the obscene Tzarist regime itself.

DOSTOEVSKY TAKES ON THE ROLE OF SOCIAL CRITIC

Yet out of his own life-long misery and isolation, his epileptic seizures, the hackwork to which he was condemned; out of the neurotic split in his personality which he tried to hide under the dubiously protective wings of the Father-Tzar and the myth of "Holy Russia," he made himself the supreme spokesman of the rebellious, the alienated, the spiritual loneliness of modern life. He thought of himself—or rather, he *liked* to think of himself—as an enemy of the liberals, of scientific advance, of the iconoclasm that threatened the foundations of the Tzarist state. But he was the greatest of all the iconoclasts himself. For he went straight to the unrevealed nature of man himself.

The greatness of Dostoevsky's work stems above all from the fearlessness, the hard swift knowledge, with which he uncovered the fictions that are conventionally used to describe human nature. And what he showed so unforgettably in *Crime and Punishment* is the long-suppressed will of man to absolute power. Raskolnikov is a man who sought to create, in his daily life, the same feeling of dominion over his own nature that Napoleon established over Europe. Raskolnikov's dream is that of conquering at any cost, of proving oneself able to conquer. The old woman he kills means nothing to him; if he hates her at all, it is because she is mean and dishonest; but the hatred is not enough for murder. *The murder is only to prove that he can do it; to prove that he is absolutely independent of morality.* As a portrait of the Russian intellectual, this is grotesque and unfair. As a portrait of our universal human weakness, of the will to prove ourselves because our lives are petty and miserable, it has a power and an immediate truth that the contemporaries of Adolf Hitler can bitterly affirm. And let us not forget that there are many Hitlers who have never come to power. The seeds of Fascist sadism and exasperated unreason are in us all. They exist wherever men are so split in themselves, wherever human relations are so barren, that they will do anything to rise out of their self-humiliation. What the psychologists so easily call "compensation," Dostoevsky made the very stuff of a man's life. He showed that man has become so lonely in the modern world, and therefore so hard, that he will carry out the logic of materialism to its human breaking point. The old woman Raskolnikov kills is only a material object to him, as in his mind the wish to kill is only a material desire. The murder, then, is the symbol of his thinking, of his revenge on his own powerlessness. It is the unalterable logic of his cutting himself off from authority, from love, from men. If we are nothing to ourselves, others are nothing to us; thus we can kill.

The crime is real enough, but its real stage is Raskolnikov's mind. And it is there that the punishment takes place. Solitude, bottomless and unreachable human solitude, sets the scene for us from the first. From the moment Raskolnikov leaves his room to plot the murder; from the moment we know that we have in him one of those men to whom an idea is more than human life, we are plunged with him into the nightmare of even greater loneliness, remorse, and delirium. Hence the extraordinarily sustained line on which the narrative is played out: everything is seen in terms of Raskolnikov's terrible solitude, and it is a world of such intense private emotions that Dostoevsky has no room for anything else. There is no view of nature here, or of the pageant of history; there is nothing of the small talk of "normal" life. We are in the mind of a man who has vowed to rise above the meanness of his days by committing a murder, and he will not be released from his guilt until he has reached the bottom-most meaning of his act. As his crime arose from his solitude, so he must suffer in solitude; the absoluteness of it is his punishment. Even when he confesses, his solitude is not broken. He confesses to release himself, just enough, to save himself from what is finally unbearable in his self-punishment and threatens him with madness. He is not even released from it by being sent to Siberia, for he has still not understood the meaning of his act. His solitude still imprisons him from human love. It is only when Sonia, the eternal Magdalene, moves him by the compelling power of her own love that his prison walls are broken down. The walls were only in him, and though he is now in prison, he is free. The murderer and the harlot sit together by a river in Siberia, and for the first time the broken halves of the self are brought together. Only then is the crime understood, and only by his power to love is the punishment over.

CHAPTER 2

The Composition and Narration of *Crime and Punishment*

Dostoyevsky's Choice of Narrative Voice

Joseph Frank

Joseph Frank, professor emeritus of comparative
literature at Princeton and Stanford universities, is
one of the foremost biographers and critics of Dostoyevsky. In this selection, he uses Dostoyevsky's own
notes on an early draft of the novel composed in
Wiesbaden, Germany, (Frank refers to it as the
"Wiesbaden version") in order to discuss the process
by which Dostoyevsky arrived at his choice of third-
person rather than first-person narration for *Crime
and Punishment*. Frank also puts the narrative style
of this book into context by briefly comparing it with
that of a number of other stylistically innovative
writers, highlighting what he sees as Dostoyevsky's
unique style characteristics.

Crime and Punishment came to birth only when, in November 1865, Dostoevsky shifted from a first-person to a third-
person narrator; and this was the culmination of a long
struggle whose vestiges can be traced all through the early
stages of composition. Some of the problems of using the
first person are already apparent from the earliest version,
whose first chapter is supposedly written five days after the
murder has taken place (on June 9). The narrator dates the
beginning of his diary as June 14 because, as he explains, to
have written anything earlier would have been impossible in
view of his mental and emotional confusion. Indeed, even
when he begins to write, this same state of confusion continues to plague him, and Dostoevsky reminds himself [in
his notebooks] to remember that in "all these six chapters
[the narrator] must write, speak, and appear to the reader in
part as if not in possession of his senses."

Dostoevsky thus wished to convey the narrator's partial

Excerpted from "The Making of *Crime and Punishment*," by Joseph Frank, in *Critical
Reconstructions: The Relationship of Fiction and Life*, edited by Robert M. Polhemus
and Roger B. Henkle, with the permission of the publishers, Stanford University Press.
Copyright ©1994 by the Board of Trustees of the Leland Stanford Junior University.

mental instability, while at the same time using him as a focus on the external world and also conveying the reactions induced in him by his crime as the action proceeds. All this posed serious difficulties, and the manuscript version shows Dostoevsky's constant uncertainty about how to hold the balance between the narrator's psychic disarray and the needs of his story. He writes, for example, in the first chapter: "I had already started up the stairs, but [suddenly] I remembered the ax. I don't understand how I could even for a single moment have forgotten about it; [it was after all necessary]. It tortures me now. It was the last pressing difficulty I had to take care of." Dostoevsky crosses out the last three sentences because they obviously show a narrator reflecting on actions that had taken place in the past; and such reflections indicate a composure that the writer was not yet supposed to have attained.

This problem of time-perspective bothered Dostoevsky from the very start, and he moves the second chapter back several more days, to June 16, in order to give his narrator more time to come to his senses; but such an expedient could only be a temporary stopgap. The distance between past and present was still not great enough, and this led to an inevitable clash between the situation in which the narrator was immersed and his function as narrator. As Edward Wasiolek has rightly pointed out, "Raskolnikov is supposed to be . . . fixed wholly on his determination to elude his imaginary pursuers. But the 'I' point of view forces him to provide his own interpretations, and, even worse, his own stylistic refinements. Every stylistic refinement wars against the realism of the dramatic action." As a result, there are serious doubts about the verisimilitude of a narrator presumably in a state of semi-hysteria who yet is able to remember and analyze, to report long scenes as well as lengthy dialogues, and in general to function as a reliable observer. This problem was only made more acute when the Marmeladovs entered the picture, and fragments of the drunkard's monologues begin to appear among the notes.

Changing from "I" to "He"

There is ample evidence that Dostoevsky was acutely aware of this issue, and the first expedient he thought of is indicated by a brief note: "The *story* ends and the *diary* begins." Since no trace of such a dual form can be found, this idea was probably abandoned very quickly; but one understands how Dostoevsky's mind was working. He wished to separate a recital of events, set down by the narrator after they had been completed, from another account of the same events written by someone still caught in their flux; this would have eliminated the disturbing clash between one and the other so noticeable in the Wiesbaden version. The same purpose inspires the next alternative, the Petersburg version, which is entitled "On Trial," and whose author is now in the custody of the legal authorities.

In this text, the narrator begins: "[I am on trial and] I will tell everything. I will write everything down. I am writing this for myself, but let others and all my judges read it, [if they want to]. This is a confession (a full confession). I am writing for myself, for my own needs and therefore I will not keep anything secret." This draft continues with Marmeladov's monologic recital of his woes (preserved almost verbatim in the eventual novel); and by this time the schema of events has been recast so that this scene clearly precedes the murder. Most important, though, is that the position of the narrator, sitting in jail and sadly contemplating his errors, allows him both to respond and to reflect without unduly straining credibility. But even in this plan, the time gap between the termination of all the events and the narrative is very small (roughly a week), and Dostoevsky remained uneasy; after all, the narrator can hardly be completely tranquil since the trial has not yet taken place.

The notebooks thus contain a third possibility, which is attached to a near-definitive outline of the action concerning Raskolnikov during the first two-thirds of the novel. "*A New Plan*," Dostoevsky announces, "*The Story of a Criminal.* Eight years before (in order to keep it completely at a distance)!" The phrase in parentheses indicates just how preoccupied Dostoevsky was with this issue of narrative distance, and how clearly he saw all of the problems involved. In this new plan, the narrator would be writing after the conclusion of his prison term (eight years), and what was probably the subtitle would indicate the profound moral alteration induced by the passage of time; the narrator now calls *himself* a criminal, no longer maintaining that the murder could not be considered a "crime" at all. In any event, the narrator is now so far removed from his previous self that it would require only a short step to shift from an I-narrator to the third person.

THE PROCESS OF SHIFTING NARRATIVE PERSON

This shift, however, did not occur all at once, and Dostoev-sky debates the reasons for it in pages that, being contiguous to those just cited, were probably written almost simultane-ously. "Rummage through all the questions in this novel," he admonishes himself, and then proceeds to do so. "If it is to be a confession," he muses, "then everything must be made clear to the *utter extreme.* Every instant of the story must be entirely clear." The recognition of this necessity leads Dos-toevsky to some second thoughts: "*For consideration.* If a confession, then in parts it will not be chaste (*tselomu-drenno*) and it will be difficult to imagine why it was writ-ten." The use of the term "chaste" in this context is rather odd; but it seems to refer to the question of why the narra-tive has been written at all. Why should the narrator have wished to engage in so lacerating an act of self-exposure? At this point, Dostoevsky comes to the conclusion that his nar-rative technique must be altered. "But the subject is like this. The story from oneself (the author), and not from *him* (the character)." What Dostoevsky means by "subject" is left am-biguous; but he may be thinking about his conception of a main character who reveals unexpected aspects of himself after the crime of which, previously, he had not been fully aware. If, in a first-person narration, "everything must be made clear *to the utter extreme*" at every instant, then it would be difficult to obtain such an effect of self-surprise; at best it could be referred to and explained, but hardly pre-sented with full dramatic impact. Taken in conjunction with the problem of justifying his narrative, such considerations would explain why Dostoevsky, despite his desperate eco-nomic straits, could not resist making a fresh start and transferring to a third-person narrator.

But there still remained the question of exactly what kind of narrator this should be. Contemporary narratologists have hailed, as a recent triumph of their discipline, the discovery that authorial narrators are not just loose, amorphous pres-ences who know how to spin a yarn; they are, rather, inte-gral parts of the text with distinct profiles and attitudes that decisively shape the novelistic perspective. Dostoevsky, as it turns out, was fully conscious of this important truth, and he tries to define exactly the stance that his authorial narrator will adopt. No such problem had arisen earlier because, since the narrator was the central character, everything had been presented from his own point of view—which meant by someone who, though guilty of a terrible crime, would inevitably arouse a certain sympathy because of his altruistic impulses, his inner sufferings, and his final repentance. What sort of third-person narrator could play the same role in relation to the reader? As Dostoevsky pondered the choice between the first and third person, he wrote: "But from *the author.* Too much naiveté and frankness are needed." Why this should be so is hardly self-evident; but Dostoevsky's elliptical notes leave open the possibility that he may still have been thinking about some sort of confessional novel which, even if cast in the third person, would involve the total identification of the narrator with the main protagonist. This would help explain the emphasis of the next sentence, which insists on the *separation* of the author from the character. "An *omniscient and faultless author* will have to be assumed, who holds up to the view of all one of the members of the new generation."

The narrator will thus be undertaking a specific historical task: to exhibit for scrutiny an example of the very latest Russian type, the successor to Bazarov [a character from Ivan Turgenev's novel *Fathers and Sons*] and the other "new men" of Russian literature. But Dostoevsky may have felt that such a narrator would be *too* coolly detached, too "omniscient and faultless" to serve his purposes ("faultless" translates the Russian *ne pogreshayuschim,* which contains the strong moral connotation of sinlessness). He therefore alters his narrator, in another notation, merely to a "sort of invisible but omniscient being, *who doesn't leave his hero for a moment,* even with the words: 'all that was done completely by chance'" (italics added). By attaching the narrator as closely as possible to the protagonist's point of view, Dostoevsky retains the advantages of I-narration, which automatically generates the effect of identification and sympathy created by all inside views of a character; and he reminds himself to maintain such inside views, as far as possible, even when moving from the direct portrayal of consciousness into summary and report. At the same time, he retains the freedom of omniscience necessary to dramatize the process of Raskolnikov's self-discovery, to reveal the character gradually, to comment on him from the outside when this becomes necessary, and to leave him entirely when the plot-action widens out.

DOSTOEVSKY'S NARRATIVE STYLE IN A WIDER CONTEXT

This narrative technique fuses the narrator very closely with the consciousness and point of view of the central character as well as other important figures (though without, as Mikhail Bakhtin was inclined to maintain, eliminating him entirely as a controlling perspective). Dostoevsky had used a similar narrative approach earlier in *The Double*, and such a fusion was by no means unprecedented in the history of the novel (in Jane Austen, among others); but in *Crime and Punishment* this identification begins to approach, through Dostoevsky's use of the time shifts of memory and his remarkable manipulation of temporal sequence, the experiments of Henry James, Joseph Conrad, and later stream-of-consciousness writers such as Virginia Woolf and James Joyce. Brilliantly original for its period, this technique gives us the superbly realized masterpiece we know, whose masterly construction and artistic sophistication can only cause us to wonder at the persistence of the legend that Dostoevsky was an untidy and negligent craftsman. Some light on this legend may be cast by the remark of E.M. de Vogüé, a novelist himself, who wrote with some surprise in 1886 of *Crime and Punishment* that "a word . . . one does not even notice, a small fact that takes up only a line, have their reverberations fifty pages later . . . [so that] the continuity becomes unintelligible if one skips a couple of pages." This acute observation, which expresses all the disarray of a late nineteenth-century reader accustomed to the more orderly and linear types of expository narration, helps to account for the tenacity of this critical misjudgment; but it has now been replaced by a more accurate appreciation of Dostoevsky's pathbreaking originality.

The Many Voices of *Crime and Punishment*

Mikhail Bakhtin

Perhaps more than any other single figure in Russian literary criticism, Mikhail Bakhtin has changed the way in which modern readers approach the work of Dostoyevsky. His book *Problems of Dostoevsky's Poetics*, from which the following selection is taken, is important not only for its insightful interpretations of Dostoyevsky's writings but for its use of innovative devices like polyphony (literally, "multivoicing") and dialogism. Both devices involve competing "voices" that contribute, literally or figuratively, to the overall narrative of the book. Bakhtin argues that certain characters in the book are so closely identified with certain philosophical movements or other ideologies that these larger abstract concepts take on a sort of voice of their own in the book, contributing to the narrative as though they were characters in the actual dialogue. Not only must the reader understand the literal words that such a character speaks in the text, but one must also "hear" the voice of the ideology that this character represents. In essence, what Bakhtin is pointing out is that one must always read between the lines to fully understand the meaning of a book. Bakhtin's elaboration of these concepts has contributed an entirely new way to critically evaluate literature in general, not just the works of Dostoyevsky.

Dostoevsky was capable of *representing a foreign (chuzhaia) idea*, while still maintaining its full meaning as an idea, and at the same time maintaining distance as well, not confirming the idea and not merging it with his own expressed ideology.

In his work the idea becomes an *object of artistic repre-*

sentation, and Dostoevsky himself became a great *artist of the idea*.

It is characteristic that the image of an artist of the idea occurred to Dostoevsky already in 1846–47, i.e. at the very beginning of his creative path. We have in mind the image of Ordynov, the hero of "The Landlady." He is a lonesome young scholar. He has his own creative system, his own unusual approach to the scientific idea:

> He was creating a system for himself; it grew within him over a period of years, and in his soul a still vague and obscure, but somehow wonderfully joyful *image of an idea* was gradually taking shape, an idea embodied in a *new, blissful form*, and that form struggled to burst out of his soul, tearing at it and tormenting it; he still timidly *sensed* its originality, its *truth* and its uniqueness: creativity was already revealing itself to his powers; it was taking form and gaining strength.

And at the end of the story:

> Perhaps a complete, original, unique idea would have been born in him. Perhaps he was destined to become an *artist in science*.

Dostoevsky was also destined to become an artist of the idea, not in science, but in literature.

What are the conditions which make the artistic representation of an idea possible for Dostoevsky?

First of all we must be reminded that the image of the idea is inseparable from the image of the person, the carrier of that idea. It is not the idea in and of itself which is the "heroine of Dostoevsky's works," as B.M. Engelgardt asserts, but *rather the man of an idea (chelovek idei)*. We must again emphasize that Dostoevsky's hero is the man of an idea; this is not a character or temperament, not a social or psychological type: the image of a *full-valued* idea has, of course, nothing to do with such externalized and finalized images of people. It would, for example, be foolish to even attempt to combine Raskolnikov's idea, which we understand and *feel* (according to Dostoevsky an idea can and must be not only understood, but "felt" as well), with his finalized character or his social typicality as a *raznochinec* [the *raznochintsy* were a class of people between the peasants and the gentry in 19th century Russia, including merchants, tradesmen, sons of clergy, etc.] of the '60's: his idea would immediately lose its direct significance as a full-valued idea and would be removed from the conflict in which it *lives* in ceaseless dialogical interaction with other full-valued ideas—those of

Sonya, Porfiry, Svidrigailov, etc. The carrier of a full-valued idea can be none other than the "man in man," with his free unfinalizedness and indeterminacy. . . . It is precisely to this unfinalized inner nucleus of Raskolnikov's personality that Sonya, Porfiry and others dialogically address themselves. It is also to this unfinalized nucleus of Raskolnikov's personality that the author, by virtue of the whole structure of his novel, addresses himself.

Consequently only the unfinalizable and inexhaustible "man in man" can become the man of an idea, whose image is combined with the image of a full-valued idea. This is the first condition of the representation of the idea in Dostoevsky.

FINDING FULFILLMENT IN "GETTING AN IDEA STRAIGHT"

But this condition contains, as it were, its inverse as well. We can say that in Dostoevsky's works man overcomes his "thingness" (*veshchnost'*) and becomes "man in man" only by entering the pure and unfinalized sphere of the idea, i.e. only by becoming the selfless man of an idea. Such are all of Dostoevsky's leading characters, i.e. all of the participants in the great dialog.

In this respect Zosima's definition of Ivan Karamazov's [from *The Brothers Karamazov*] personality is applicable to all of these characters. Zosima of course couched his definition in his theological language, i.e. it stemmed from that sphere of the Christian idea in which he lived. We shall quote the appropriate passage from that—for Dostoevsky—very characteristic *penetrant (proniknovennyi)* dialog between the Elder Zosima and Ivan Karamazov.

> "Is that really your conviction regarding the consequences of the whithering of people's faith in the immortality of their souls?" the Elder Zosima asked Ivan suddenly.
>
> "Yes, I have asserted that. If there is no immortality, there is no virtue."
>
> "You are blissfully happy if you really believe that. Or terribly unhappy."
>
> "Why unhappy?" smiled Ivan.
>
> "Because in all probability you do not yourself believe either in the immortality of your soul, nor in the things that you have written about the church and the religious question."
>
> "Perhaps you are right! . . . But nonetheless it was not all merely a jest . . . ," suddenly admitted Ivan strangely, blushing quickly, by the way.

"Verily, it was not all merely a jest. *This idea is not yet resolved in your heart, and it torments you.* But he who is tormented is also fond at times of amusing himself with his despair, as if also out of despair. For the time being you, too, are amusing yourself with your despair—and with newspaper articles and worldly arguments, without yourself believing in your dialectic, under your breath laughing at it with pain in your heart. . . . *This question is unresolved in you, and that is your great misfortune, for it persistently demands a resolution. . . .*"

"But perhaps it is already resolved? Resolved in a positive direction?" Ivan continued to ask strangely, gazing steadily at the elder with some sort of inexplicable smile.

"If it cannot be resolved in a positive direction, it will never be resolved in a negative one, either; you yourself know this characteristic of your heart. Therein lies all its torment. But thank the Creator for giving you an *extraordinary heart, a heart capable of suffering such sufferings,* of '*setting its mind on things above, not on things on the earth, seeking those things which are above,* for our home is in the kingdom of heaven.' May God grant that the resolution of your heart come while you are still on earth, and may God bless your path!"

In his discussion with Rakitin Alyosha defines Ivan similarly, only in worldly language.

"Ach, Misha, his soul [Ivan's—M.B.] is a stormy one. His mind is held captive. He is filled with a great and unresolved idea. *He is one of those who don't need millions, they just need to get an idea straight.*"

All of Dostoevsky's leading characters have the capacity to "set their minds on things above" and to "seek those things which are above;" each of them is filled with a "great and unresolved idea," all of them must above all "get an idea straight." And in this resolution of an idea lies their entire real life and their personal unfinalizedness. If one were to think away the idea in which they live, their image would be totally destroyed. In other words, the image of the hero is inseparably linked with the image of the idea. We *see* the hero in and through the idea, and we *see* the idea in and through the hero. All of Dostoevsky's leading characters, as people of an idea, are absolutely unselfish, in so far as the idea has in fact taken command of the deepest core of their personality. This unselfishness is not a trait of their objective character and not an external description of their actions; unselfishness expresses their real life in the sphere of the idea (they "don't need millions, they just need to get an idea straight"). Living an idea (*ideinost*) is somehow synonymous with unselfishness. In this sense even Raskolnikov is absolutely un-selfish when he kills and robs the old woman usurer, as is the prostitute Sonya and the accomplice in the murder of Ivan Karamazov's father; the "raw youth's" *idea* to become a Rothschild is also absolutely unselfish. We repeat again: the important thing is not the ordinary classification of a person's character and actions, but rather the indicator of the dedication of his whole personality to the idea.

Dostoevsky and Dialogism of Ideas

The second condition for the creation of the image of the idea in Dostoevsky is his profound understanding of the dialogical nature of human thought, the dialogical nature of the idea. Dostoevsky was able to see, reveal and depict the true sphere of the life of an idea. An idea does not *live* in one person's *isolated* individual consciousness—if it remains there it degenerates and dies. An idea begins to live, i.e. to take shape, to develop, to find and renew its verbal expression, and to give birth to new ideas only when it enters into genuine dialogical relationships with other, *foreign*, ideas. Human thought becomes genuine thought, i.e. an idea, only under the conditions of a living contact with another foreign thought, embodied in the voice of another person, that is, in the consciousness of another person as expressed in his word. It is in the point of contact of these voice-consciousnesses that the idea is born and has its life.

The idea, as *seen* by Dostoevsky the artist, is not a subjective individual-psychological formulation with a "permanent residence" in a person's head; no, the idea is interindividual and intersubjective. The sphere of its existence is not the individual consciousness, but the dialogical intercourse *between* consciousnesses. The idea is a *living event* which is played out in the point where two or more consciousnesses meet dialogically. In this respect the idea resembles the *word*, with which it forms a dialogical unity. Like the word, the idea wants to be heard, understood and "answered" by other voices from other positions. Like the word, the idea is by nature dialogical, the monolog being merely the conventional form of its expression which arose from the soil of the ideological monologism of modern times, as characterized above.

Dostoevsky saw and artistically represented the *idea* as precisely such a living event, played out between consciousness-voices. The artistic revelation of the dialogical nature of the idea, the consciousness, and of every human life that is illuminated by a consciousness (and therefore is at least marginally acquainted with ideas) made Dostoevsky a great artist of the idea.

Dostoevsky never sets forth completed ideas in monological form, but neither does he depict their *psychological* evolution within a *single* individual consciousness. In both cases the ideas would cease to be living images.

We recall, for example, Raskolnikov's first interior monolog. Here we find no psychological evolution of the idea within a *single* self-enclosed consciousness. On the contrary, the consciousness of the solitary Raskolnikov becomes the field of battle for the voices of others; the events of recent days (his mother's letter, the meeting with Marmeladov), reflected in his consciousness, take on the form of an intense dialog with absentee interlocutors (with his sister, his mother, Sonya, and others), and in this dialog he, too, seeks to "get his ideas straight."

Already before the action of the novel begins, Raskolnikov has published a newspaper article containing an exposition of the theoretical bases of his idea. Dostoevsky nowhere gives us this article in monological form. We first become acquainted with its content, and consequently with Raskolnikov's main idea, in Raskolnikov's tense and, for him, terrible, dialog with Porfiry (Razumikhin and Zametov also participate in the dialog). Porfiry is the first to give an account of the article, and he does so in a deliberately exaggerated and provocative form. This internally dialogized account is constantly interrupted by questions put to Raskolnikov, and by the replies of the latter. Then Raskolnikov himself describes his article, but he is constantly interrupted by Porfiry's provocative questions and remarks. And, from the point of view of Porfiry and his like, Raskolnikov's account is saturated with inner polemics. Razumikhin also gives his comments. As a result, Raskolnikov's idea appears before us in the interindividual zone of intense struggle between several individual consciousnesses, while the idea's theoretical side is indissolubly combined in the ultimate life-principles of the dialog's participants.

This same idea of Raskolnikov appears again in his no less tense dialogs with Sonya; here it takes on a different tonality, entering into dialogical contact with another very strong and integral life-principle, that of Sonya, thus revealing new facets and potentialities. Next we hear this idea in Svidrigailov's dialogized presentation in his conversation with Dunya. But in the voice of Svidrigailov, who is one of Raskolnikov's parodical doubles, the idea has a completely different sound, and it turns another of its sides toward us. And lastly, Raskolnikov's idea comes into contact throughout the entire novel with various manifestations of life, it is

AN EXAMPLE OF BAKHTIN'S THEORY AT WORK

One of the more explicit instances of "dialogism" that Bakhtin points out in Crime and Punishment *is the conversation in Chapter V of Book Three between Raskolnikov, Porfiry, Razumikhin, and Zamyotov on the subject of Raskolnikov's article. Note the way in which the ideas of the article are always presented in second-hand form and in conflicting ways by the various speakers.*

"So you still believe in the New Jerusalem?"

"I believe," Raskolnikov answered firmly; saying this, as throughout his whole tirade, he looked at the ground, having picked out a certain spot on the carpet.

"And . . . and . . . and do you also believe in God? Excuse me for being so curious."

"I believe," Raskolnikov repeated, looking up at Porfiry.

"And . . . and do you believe in the raising of Lazarus?"

"I be-believe. What do you need all this for?"

"You believe literally?"

"Literally."

"I see, sir . . . just curious. Excuse me, sir. But if I may say so—returning to the previous point—they aren't always punished; some, on the contrary . . ."

"Triumph in their own lifetime? Oh, yes, some attain in their own lifetime, and then . . ."

"Start doing their own punishing?"

"If necessary, and, in fact, almost always. Your observation, generally speaking is quite witty."

"Thank you, sir. But tell me this: how does one manage to distinguish those extraordinary ones from the ordinary? Are they somehow marked at birth, or what? What I'm getting at is that one could do with more accuracy here, more outward certainty, so to speak: excuse the natural uneasiness of a practical and law-abiding man, but wouldn't it be possible, in this case, to introduce some special clothing, the wearing of some insignia or whatever? . . . Because, you must agree, if there is some sort of mix-up, and a person from one category imagines tried and tested, and it is confirmed or refuted by them. . . .

Let us also recall Ivan Karamazov's idea that "everything is permissible" ("*vse pozvoleno*") as long as the soul is not immortal. What an intense dialogical life this idea lives throughout the entire novel *The Brothers Karamazov*! What a variety of voices expresses it and what unexpected dialogical contacts it makes!

---

he belongs to the other category and starts 'removing all obstacles,' as you quite happily put it, well then . . ."

"Oh, it happens quite often! This observation is even wittier than your last one. . . ."

"Thank you, sir. . . ."

"Not at all, sir; but consider also that a mistake is possible only on the part of the first category, that is the 'ordinary' people (as I have called them, perhaps rather unfortunately). In spite of their innate tendency to obedience, by some playful nature that is not denied even to cows, quite a few of them like to imagine themselves progressive people, 'destroyers,' who are in on the 'new word,' and that in all sincerity, sir.". . .

"What, are you two joking or something?" Razumikhin cried out at last. "Addling each other's brain aren't you? Sitting there and poking fun at each other! Are you serious, Rodya?"

Raskolnikov silently raised his pale, almost sad face to him, and did not answer. And how strange this quiet and sad face seemed to Razumikhin next to the undisguised, intrusive, annoying and *impolite* sarcasm of Porfiry.

"Well, brother, if it's really serious then. . . . You're right, of course, in saying that it's nothing new, and resembles everything we've read and heard a hundred times over; but what is indeed *original* in it all—and to my horror, is really yours alone—is that you do finally permit bloodshed *in all conscience* and, if I may say so, even with such fanaticism. . . . So this is the main point of your article. This permission to shed blood *in all conscience* is . . . is to my mind more horrible than if bloodshed were officially, legally permitted. . . ."

"Quite right, it's more horrible," Porfiry echoed.

"No, you got carried away somehow! It's a mistake. I'll read it. . . . You got carried away! You can't think like that. . . . I'll read it."

"That's not all in the article; it's only hinted at," said Raskolnikov.

Excerpted from Fyodor Dostoyevsky, *Crime and Punishment* (translated by Richard Pevear and Larissa Volokhonsky). New York: Alfred A. Knopf, 1993, pp. 261–62.

Both of these ideas (Raskolnikov's and Ivan Karamazov's) reflect other ideas, just as in painting a certain color, because of the reflections of the surrounding colors, loses its abstract purity, but in return begins to live a truly colorful life. If one were to withdraw these ideas from the dialogical sphere of their lives and give them a monologically completed theoretical form, what cachetic and easily-refuted ideological constructions would result!

THE SOURCES FOR SOME OF DOSTOEVSKY'S "VOICES"

As an artist Dostoevsky did not create his ideas in the same way that philosophers and scholars create theirs—he created living images of the ideas which he found, detected, or sometimes divined in *reality itself,* i.e. images of already living ideas, ideas already existing as idea-forces. Dostoevsky possessed a brilliant gift for hearing the dialog of his age, or, more precisely, for perceiving his age as a great dialog, and for capturing in it not only individual voices, but above all the *dialogical relationships* between voices, their dialogical *interaction.* He heard both the dominant, recognized, loud voices of the age, that is to say, the dominant, leading ideas (both official and unofficial), and the still-weak voices, the ideas which had not yet reached full development, the latent ideas which no one else had yet discerned, and the ideas which were only beginning to mature, the embryos of future *Weltanschauungen* [German phrase meaning "world-view"]. Dostoevsky himself wrote: "Reality is not limited to the familiar, the commonplace, for it consists in huge part of a *latent, as yet unspoken future Word.*"

In the dialog of his times Dostoevsky heard the resonances of the voice-ideas of the past, too—both of the recent past (the 1830s and 40s), and of the more remote. He also strove, as we have just said, to discern the voice-ideas of the future, seeking to divine them, so to speak, in the place prepared for them in the dialog of the present, in the same way that it is possible to foresee a reply which has not yet been uttered in a dialog which is already in progress. Thus, the past, the present, and the future came together and confronted one another in the plane of contemporaneity.

We repeat: Dostoevsky never created his idea-images out of nothing, he never "invented" them, any more than a painter invents the people he paints; he was able to hear and divine them in existing reality. Therefore it is possible to find

and point out the specific *prototypes* of the ideas in Dostoev-
sky's novels, as well as those of his heroes. The prototypes of
Raskolnikov's ideas, for example, were the ideas of Max
Sterner as expressed in his tract "Der Einzige und sein
Eigentum," and the ideas of Napoleon III, developed in his
book *Histoire de Jules César* (1865); one of the prototypes for
Petr Verkhovensky's ideas was *Catechism of a Revolutionary;*
the prototypes of Versilov's ideas (in *A Raw Youth*) were the
ideas of Chaadaev and Herzen. Not all of the prototypes for
Dostoevsky's idea-images have as yet been discovered. We
must emphasize that we are not referring here to Dostoevsky's "sources"—that term would be inappropriate—but
precisely to the *prototypes* of his images of ideas.

Dostoevsky in no way copied or expounded on these prototypes; he freely and creatively re-worked them into living
artistic images of ideas, in the very same way that an artist
works with his human prototypes. Above all, he destroyed
the self-enclosed monological form of his idea-prototypes
and made them part of the great dialog of his novels, where
they begin to live a new, eventful artistic life.

As an artist, Dostoevsky revealed in the image of a given
idea not only the actual and historical traits which were present in the prototype (in Napoleon's *Histoire de Jules César*,
for example), but its *potentialities* as well, and it is just these
potentialities that are of prime importance for an artistic image. Dostoevsky often made artistic conjectures as to how a
given idea would develop and behave under certain altered
conditions, or as to the unexpected directions its further development and transformation would take. For this purpose
Dostoevsky placed the idea at the vertex of dialogically in-
tersecting consciousnesses. He brought together ideas and
Weltanschauungen which were in real life completely divergent and deaf to one another, and caused them to dispute. He
as it were extended these ideas by means of a dotted line to
their point of intersection. Thus he anticipated the future
convergence of ideas which were as yet divergent. He fore-
saw new combinations of ideas, the emergence of new idea-
voices, and changes in the arrangement of all the idea-
voices in the universal dialog. This is why the Russian—and
universal—dialog of Dostoevsky's works, a dialog of al-
ready-living idea-voices with idea-voices that are still being
born, that are still unfinalized and fraught with new possibilities, continues to involve the minds and voices of Dosto-

evsky's readers in its tragic and exalted game.

Thus the idea-prototypes used in Dostoevsky's novels alter the form of their existence, without losing the significance of their meaning: they become completely dialogized, not monologically finalized, images of ideas, i.e. they enter a new sphere of *artistic* existence.

Dostoevsky was not only an artist who wrote novels and stories, but also a publicist-thinker who published articles in *Vremia, Epoxa, Grazhdanin* and *Dnevnik pisatelia* (*Time, The Epoch, The Citizen* and *Diary of a Writer*). In those articles he expressed specific philosophical, religious-philosophical, social-political, and other ideas; in the articles he expressed *his own confirmed* ideas in *systematic-monological* or rhetorical-monological (i.e. *publicistic*) form. He sometimes expressed the same ideas in letters to various people. Here, in the articles and letters, he gives, of course, not images of ideas, but direct, monologically confirmed ideas.

But we meet these "Dostoevskian ideas" in his novels as well. How should we regard them there, i.e. in the artistic context of his creative work?

In exactly the same way as we regard Napoleon III's ideas in *Crime and Punishment* (ideas with which Dostoevsky the thinker was totally at variance), or the ideas of Chaadaev and Herzen in *A Raw Youth* (ideas with which Dostoevsky the thinker was in partial agreement); i.e. we should regard the ideas of Dostoevsky the thinker as *idea-prototypes* for certain idea-images in his novels (the images of the ideas of Sonya, Myshkin, Alyosha Karamazov, Zosima).

Actually, the ideas of Dostoevsky the thinker change the very form of their existence when they become part of his polyphonic novel; they are turned into artistic images of ideas: they become indissoluably combined with the images of people (Sonya, Myshkin, Zosima), they are freed from their monological isolation and finalization, becoming completely dialogized and entering into the great dialog of the novel *on completely equal terms* with other idea-images (the ideas of Raskolnikov, Ivan Karamazov and others). It is totally inadmissable to ascribe to them the finalizing function of the author's ideas in a monological novel. As equal participants in the great dialog, they simply do not have such a function. If a certain partiality of Dostoevsky the publicist for various ideas or images is sometimes felt in the novels, it is manifested only in superficial ways (as in the conventional-monological epilogue to *Crime and Punishment*, for example) and cannot destroy the powerful artistic logic of the polyphonic novel. Dostoevsky the artist always wins out over Dostoevsky the publicist.

Thus Dostoevsky's private ideas, expressed in monological form outside the artistic context for his work (in articles, letters and conversations), are only the prototypes of certain images of ideas in his novels. For this reason it is totally inadmissable to substitute a criticism of these monological idea-prototypes for a genuine analysis of Dostoevsky's polyphonic artistic thought. It is important that the *function* of ideas in Dostoevsky's polyphonic world be revealed, and not only their *monological substance.*

The Power of Words in *Crime and Punishment*

Thomas Werge

Thomas Werge, a professor of English at Notre Dame University, approaches *Crime and Punishment* from a partially theological perspective. Werge argues that both Raskolnikov's crime and his possible redemption are prefigured by what he calls "performative utterances" (i.e., words that take the place of actual deeds or make such deeds inevitable). Werge relies heavily on a comparison between the earthly "new word" that Raskolnikov seeks for much of the book, and the "Word" of Scripture that Sonya reads to him.

One of the most striking aspects of Dostoyevsky's emphasis in *Crime and Punishment* on the reality and power of language is his consistent awareness of an opposing interpretation of language. Throughout the narrative, his characters indicate that words are random noises, or purely aesthetic, but ultimately amoral and meaningless. Early in the work, for example, Raskolnikov's mother defines "deed" in the ordinary language sense as an action or performance which is often contrasted to words. Raskolnikov's sister Dounia, she writes in a letter to him, has told her that "'words are not deeds,' and that, of course is perfectly true." As Raskolnikov speaks with someone in a tavern about the theoretical justification for murdering the old woman he finally does kill, his companion replies, "You are talking and speechifying away, but tell me, would you kill the old woman *yourself*?" Raskolnikov's answer divorces word from deed and rhetoric from reality: "Of course not! I was only arguing the justice of it. . . . It's nothing to do with me." Even the detective Porfiry seems oblivious to the profound implications of Raskolnikov's article—in which Raskolnikov has proclaimed the right of the "extraordinary man" to shed innocent blood in his quest

Excerpted from Thomas Werge, "The Word as Deed in *Crime and Punishment*," *Renascence: Essays on Values in Literature*, vol. 27, no. 4 (Summer 1975), pp. 208–15. Reprinted by permission of *Renascence*.

for freedom and power—and only interested in the article as a "literary amateur" and from "a literary point of view."

Yet each of these apparent negations of the power of the word in fact reinforces Dostoyevsky's affirmation of that power and efficacy. The truism that "words are not deeds" is undermined by our knowledge that neither Raskolnikov's mother, who agrees with the statement, nor Dounia, who utters it, nor Raskolnikov, who reads it, believes it for a moment. For Dounia, the truism is a transparent rationalization. She utters it only because she has been wounded by the cutting words of her wealthy but repulsive suitor. Her defensive remark that words are not deeds becomes grotesquely ironic in light of the obvious suffering inflicted on her specifically by his words—a suffering of which her mother remains painfully aware. Raskolnikov himself is obsessed by single words in his mother's letter. He is enraged by reading that the suitor "seems" to be a kind man. Indeed, the very act of reading the letter transforms him: "While he read the letter, [his] face was wet with tears; but when he finished it, his face was pale and distorted and a bitter, wrathful and malignant smile was on his lips. . . . His heart was beating violently, and his brain was in a turmoil."

Dostoyevsky's dramatic and intense language here is the culmination of his equally intense description of Raskolnikov as he receives the letter. The letter seems not only to be a portent but to be possessed of a soul. Raskolnikov cries out to the girl who tells him of its arrival, "A letter? for me! from whom? . . . bring it to me, for God's sake, bring it . . . good God!"

> He turned pale when he took it. . . . The letter was quivering in his hand; he did not want to open it in her presence; he wanted to be left *alone* with this letter . . . he lifted it quickly to his lips and kissed it; then he gazed intently at the address, the small, sloping handwriting, so dear and familiar, of the mother who had once taught him to read and write. He delayed; he seemed almost afraid of something. At last he opened it.

Similarly, Raskolnikov is able to assert that his speech in the tavern about the murder was "ordinary" rhetoric. But the apparent distinction between word and deed again proves deceptive when Raskolnikov realizes that "he had just come from [the pawnbroker] and here at once heard her name" mentioned in the tavern:

> why had he happened to hear such a discussion and such ideas at the very moment when his own brain was just con-

ceiving . . . *the very same ideas*? And why, just at the moment when he had brought away the embryo of his idea from the old woman had he dropped at once upon a conversation about her? This coincidence always seemed strange to him. This trivial talk in a tavern had an immense influence on him in his later action; as though there had really been in it something preordained, some guiding hint.

The efficacy of the words of the letter and conversation testifies to Raskolnikov's—and to Dostoyevsky's—conviction of the essential bond between language and reality, word and deed.

WORDS LEAD TO DEEDS

Yet it is Raskolnikov's preoccupation with his own "word" that illuminates most starkly Dostoyevsky's insistence that the bond between word and deed is finally an absolute bond. Raskolnikov is obsessed by mankind's need, and especially his own need, "to utter a new word." The first time we see him, he speculates that man fears more than anything else "taking a new step, uttering a new word." He later asserts that those the world calls criminals are in fact "great men or even men a little out of the common, that is to say capable of giving some new word." For Raskolnikov there are only those who are mute and those who declare and proclaim: "I only believe," he states, "in my leading idea that men are *in general* divided by a law of nature into two categories, inferior (ordinary), that is . . . mankind that serves only to reproduce its kind, and men who have the gift or the talent to utter *a new word*." And those who have new ideas and "the faintest capacity for saying something *new*" he concludes, are "extremely few in number, extraordinarily so in fact."

It is especially significant that Raskolnikov forcefully utters and makes incarnate through the written word of his article his inner preoccupation with this new word of power, freedom, and, ultimately, destruction. In light of our knowledge and Porfiry's knowledge of the potency and force of Raskolnikov's isolated will and of the nature of his intention, Porfiry's comment that he is interested in Raskolnikov's article merely "from a literary point of view"—a comment Raskolnikov sees as insolent—is profoundly ironic. Indeed, Porfiry makes clear to Raskolnikov that the article has not only contributed to but is the cause of his suspicion that Raskolnikov has committed the murder: "I thought . . . of your article in that journal, do you remember, on your first visit we talked of it? I jeered at you at the time, but that was only to lead you on . . . your article seemed familiar to me." He again states ironically that "as a literary amateur, I am awfully fond of such first essays, full of the heat of youth." But he finally concludes with what to us must be utter seriousness, "I read your article and put it aside, thinking as I did so 'that man won't go the common way.' Well, I ask you, after that as a preliminary, how could I help being carried away by what followed?" For Porfiry, here and later in the narrative, the "evidence" and "testimony" of the article are far more crucial to his suspicion of Raskolnikov than the apparently damaging circumstantial evidence that implicates other suspects Porfiry refuses to take seriously—even when one of those suspects confesses to the murder.

Porfiry reads, experiences, and apprehends Raskolnikov's article, then, not in any aesthetic or purely "literary" way. The article is not . . . a structure of empty sounds, arbitrary phonemes, or even signs. Raskolnikov's article is the declaration of his intent and will. As Porfiry describes the article, he surely could as easily be describing the conception and deed of the murder of the pawnbroker. That is, in the following sentences the word "crime" could replace the word "article" without affecting the tone and essence of Porfiry's argument. The article, he states to Raskolnikov, was "conceived on sleepless nights, with a throbbing heart, in ecstasy and suppressed enthusiasm. And that proud suppressed enthusiasm in young people is dangerous. . . . It's a gloomy article."

> Your article is absurd and fantastic, but there's a transparent sincerity, a youthful incorruptible pride and the daring of despair in it.

Through the utterance of his intent and will in the act of writing, Raskolnikov commits a deed that is itself murderous. His written word becomes the ground of his later crime; the two are as closely linked as the murder and the punishment, or guilt, that follows it. Raskolnikov's words possess causal power. His article is an incantatory and self-fulfilling prophecy rather than a theory. Once uttered, his article necessarily makes his later crime inevitable.

In light of the intensity of Raskolnikov's imagination and the world of *Crime and Punishment*, it may even be misleading to refer to a "later" crime than the "crime" of the act of writing the article. A chronological sequence of written word and murderous act certainly exists; yet this particular word is itself murderous as it is clear that Raskolnikov sees the act of murder as part of his "new word." The sequence is simultaneous rather than separated in psychological or ontological space and time. Even if we speak of the act of writing as "analogous" to the act of murder, we must emphasize the similarity, indeed the identity, of the two acts. For Dostoyevsky conceives at least two conventionally different objects, ideas, and processes—pen and axe, writing and killing—as "essentially" the same. Raskolnikov's pen is the instrument of his will. It gives birth to and seals the reality of the literal axe. In one sense, the pen is more potent and frightening than the axe, for its lethal consequences are generated by the "mere words" which some could never admit to the status or reality of actual deeds. But for Raskolnikov and Porfiry the utterance is neither abstract nor theoretical. It is a promise, a declaration, a vow, and a commissive deed. Through it, Raskolnikov proclaims, names, and wills his world and in so doing commits an act as crucial to Dostoyevsky's narrative as the murder itself. This is not to argue, of course, for the irrelevancy of the murder; the shedding of blood and the taking of flesh and life is the way in which Raskolnikov "makes his word flesh." Raskolnikov interprets the murder as the fulfillment of his "new word." But the written utterance by which Raskolnikov declares his intent is the deed from which the murder is generated. Without it, the murder would not and could not take place.

"ILLOCUTIONARY ACTS": HOW WORDS CAN *BE* DEEDS

Dostoyevsky's conviction of the power of the word—here, of course, the word used for destruction—ultimately rests on religious presuppositions concerning the nature and origins of language. J.L. Austin's more strictly philosophical analysis in *How To Do Things with Words* of a certain use of language also may help to illuminate Raskolnikov's word-deed. Austin argues that we cannot simply contrast doing and saying, deed and utterance. Even apart from the obvious fact that in stating x one is performing the act of uttering words, he insists, there are crucial uses of language in which "the issuing of the utterance" *is itself,* "the performing of an action—it is not . . . thought of as just saying something." Austin calls such utterances "illocutionary acts," or, more specifically, "performative utterances." The declarations "I do" as uttered in the marriage ritual, "I name this ship the *Queen Elizabeth*" as uttered in the ritual of commissioning, "I baptize you . . ."

as uttered in the baptismal rite, and "I promise" as uttered on any occasion, are performative utterances. Austin states of the declaration "I do," which serves to represent all such performatives:

> Here we should say that in saying these words we are *doing* something—namely, marrying, rather than *reporting* something, namely *that* we are marrying. And the act of marrying . . . is at least *preferably* . . . to be described as *saying certain words*, rather than as performing a different, inward and spiritual, action of which these words are merely the outward and audible sign.

Raskolnikov's word and article constitute precisely such a performative utterance. His word *enacts* its own reality and meaning rather than referring abstractly to them.

Austin's description of this performative use of language is central to our understanding of the relationship between Porfiry and Raskolnikov. Porfiry knows that Raskolnikov conceives himself to be one of those precious few who are capable of uttering a new word. Immediately before he asks Raskolnikov whether he would be willing, whatever the motive, to steal and murder, Porfiry seeks with apparent but ironic reluctance to express "a little notion." When Raskolnikov seems impatient with his coyness, Porfiry replies, "Well, you see . . . I really don't know how to express it properly. . . . It's a playful, psychological idea."

> "*When you were writing your article* [italics mine], surely you couldn't have helped, he-he, fancying yourself . . . just a little, an 'extraordinary' man, uttering a *new word* in your sense. . . . That's so, isn't it?"

> "Quite possibly," Raskolnikov answered contemptuously.

Raskolnikov's response clearly results from his recognition of the undeniable truth of Porfiry's claim. His contempt is in fact assent.

Dostoyevsky's conception of language as intensely real, compelling, and efficacious militates against the notion that words are "signs" in the narrowest sense and purely aesthetic in purpose. It also contends against the repudiation of verbal language by the nineteenth-century revolutionaries and nihilists with whom Dostoyevsky was associated before his arrest, his last-minute pardon from execution, his suffering in prison, and his exile. The anarchist or nihilist rejects words as unreal and meaningless. Hence he necessarily views such collective "words" and documents as Constitu-

tions, for example, as nothing more than "pieces of paper."
Since existence consists solely of naked and autonomous
wills, there is no bond of assent on which any common language or meaning can rest. Language itself cannot provide a
bond of meaning. The stark alternative, then, is "propaganda
by the deed"—acts of assassination, bombing, and terror, all
of which are lethal and non-verbal. Such acts provide the
only efficacious means by which reality can be changed and
transformed. It is especially significant, then, that Raskolnikov, whose nihilism is often overpowering, commits a
deed of murder which is so closely bound to the word of his
murderous utterance. Raskolnikov's friend Razumihin is ap-
palled by his article not simply because Raskolnikov sanctions acts of bloodshed but because he sanctions them in the
"name" of his new and self-willed "conscience" and word.

> "Well, brother, if you are really serious. . . . You are right . . .
> in saying that it's not new . . . but what is really original in all
> this, and is exclusively your own, to my horror, is that you
> sanction bloodshed *in the name of conscience.* . . . That, I take
> it, is the point of your article. But that sanction of bloodshed
> *by conscience* is . . . more terrible than the official . . . sanction
> of bloodshed. . . . You must have exaggerated! There is some
> mistake, I shall read it. You can't think that! I shall read it."

Despite Razumihin's hope that "there is some mistake," of
course, he is clearly aware of the portentous implications of
the words Raskolnikov has written. In *How To Do Things
With Words*, Austin insists that "accuracy and morality alike
are on the side of the plain saying that *our word is our
bond.*" Razumihin's frantic tone is compelled by his knowledge that Raskolnikov's word is not abstract but a profound
and palpable bond.

   Throughout the narrative and especially in its resolution,
it is Sonia who in her faith and love prevents the triumph of
Raskolnikov's nihilism and despair. She brings to him, as
Beatrice does to Dante [in *The Divine Comedy*], the redemptive word he seeks elsewhere. Indeed, Sonia's simplicity—
often expressed in silence or in such silent gestures as attending him in his suffering, or simply holding his hand—
makes possible for him a knowledge and peace that transcend words: "Not a word passed between Raskolnikov and
her . . . but both knew [her devotion] would be [complete]."
As he begins to experience the workings of redemption,
"they wanted to speak, but could not" for joy.

   Although Sonia represents and often points to a reality beyond language, she consistently does so in words of the greatest power and efficacy. It is she who reads to a fearfully intense Raskolnikov the story of the raising of Lazarus—a story in whose literal truth Sonia completely believes. Raskolnikov, who has stated that he believes the story, is without question obsessed with it. As Sonia reads the literal Biblical words, writes Dostoyevsky, "She was trembling in a real physical fever. . . . She was getting near the story of the greatest miracle and a feeling of immense triumph came over her. Her voice rang out like a bell; triumph and joy gave it power. The lines danced before her eyes, but she knew what she was reading by heart":

> "And Jesus lifted up his eyes and said, Father, I thank Thee that Thou hast heard Me.
>
> And I knew that Thou hearest Me always; but because of the people which stand by I said it, that they may believe that Thou hast sent Me.
>
> And when He thus had spoken, He cried with a loud voice, Lazarus, come forth.
>
> And he that was dead came forth."

Sonia reads the words "loudly," Dostoyevsky states, "cold and trembling with ecstasy, as though she were seeing it before her eyes."

PERFORMATIVE ACTS IN A RELIGIOUS CONTEXT

Dostoyevsky's emphasis on speaking, hearing, and, indeed, seeing in the Biblical passage and in his description of Sonia is extremely important. The words of Christ's command and the resurrection of Lazarus effected by those words exemplify the absolute bond between word and deed throughout the Scripture. Donald D. Evans, who draws on Austin's descriptive language to good effect states [in *The Logic of Self-Involvement*], "The idea of Jesus as the 'Word' of God is of special logical interest in that His life, passion, resurrection and ascension could be interpreted as actions which have a 'performative force' and 'causal power' like words. It is as if God in the deeds of Jesus, *said*, 'I hereby adopt you as sons and decree that you are brothers'; and *said*, 'Become like this man Jesus.'" The words of the story become animate for Sonia because the deed of the raising of Lazarus is accomplished by the word of Christ's utterance and finally *becomes itself* the "Word" whose palpable reality she so clearly sees and hears. Sonia fervently believes in this reality; utters it in her incantatory reading; and exemplifies it by her life.

This "old word" of sin, suffering, death, grace, and resurrection constitutes for Sonia the reality and word that are perennially new. But if she is an instrument of grace and resurrection who becomes for Raskolnikov the word made flesh, her suffering is as constant and intense as that of any other character in the narrative. Her life vindicates Porfiry's declaration to Raskolnikov: "Do you know . . . the force of the word 'suffering' among some of these people! It's not a question of suffering for some one's benefit, but simply, 'one must suffer.'" Sonia, of course, suffers for her family and for Raskolnikov. But she is also "one [who] must suffer" in the knowledge that without suffering there can be no redemption.

Because Sonia's faith is sustained in suffering, then, it is only she who may rightfully *declare* to Raskolnikov the deed he must perform and the words he must utter before his redemption can be hoped for: "Go to the cross roads, bow down to the people, kiss the earth, for you have sinned against it too, and say aloud to the whole world, 'I am a murderer.'" It is significant that just before he attempts to act on her words, Raskolnikov recalls them in the form of a single exhortation—Sonia's "word." When he is able to find the cross roads, to bow to the people, and to kiss the earth, however, the taunts and exclamations of the crowd prevent him from enacting the fourth necessary and culminating deed, that is, the deed of his utterance: "the words, 'I am a murderer,' which were perhaps on the point of dropping from his lips, died away." But when he finally is able to confess—after first failing to speak and then making incoherent sounds—Raskolnikov's confession becomes his "new word." As an utterance—"*It was I killed the old pawnbroker woman and her sister Lizaveta with an axe and robbed them*"—it is as actively efficacious and performative in its effect as his article. Raskolnikov's confessional utterance is the only fully italicized complete sentence in the entire novel. It constitutes his self-recognition and his willingness to describe himself brutally but honestly as a "murderer" rather than romantically as an "extraordinary man." His utterance binds him to the human world and moral order he has violated. With his confessional utterance, old to Sonia but strangely new to Raskolnikov, and with the final line, "Raskolnikov repeated his statement," we at once end his "old story" and begin in

Siberia and the epilogue the "new story" of his redemption.

Through Sonia's presence as a word of grace and her use of language, Dostoyevsky makes clear that the most crucial conflict is not between the word and its absence. One of her most silent gestures occurs in the epilogue when she gives Raskolnikov, in simple humility, her copy of the New Testament: "[the book] was the one from which she had read the raising of Lazarus to him. At first he was afraid that she . . . would talk about the gospel and pester him with books. But to his great surprise she had not once approached the subject and had not even offered him the Testament. He had asked her for it himself not long before his illness and she brought him the book without a word." Sonia's silence crystallizes the presence of the Word. The conflict, then, is not between word and no word; it is the conflict between the *kinds* of word man utters, hears, and obeys that remains for Dostoyevsky the crucial question. If words are pernicious—as they are when Raskolnikov utters and submits to the reality of his article and in so doing generates the murder that inexorably follows, they are also redemptive—as when Sonia submits to the reality of the Lazarus whose story she reads, and Raskolnikov submits to the reality of the confession he utters.

The ability of Raskolnikov and mankind to submit to the word of confession and grace depends, of course, on the conversion of the will. As Evans states of the divine word-deed in Scripture, "the performative and causal efficacy of the 'utterance' depends on the response of men; it depends on whether men acknowledge the new . . . word of command, and whether men allow themselves to be influenced by the divine power." The profound mystery of freedom and predestination in Dostoyevsky precludes an easy use of the reflexive form "men *allow themselves* . . ." here. Nonetheless, Evans' statement concerning the will is especially germane to Raskolnikov. Before his conversion Raskolnikov desires only to utter a word and not to listen to one. He asserts and does not hear. Even after *commanding* Sonia to read him the story of Lazarus—"Find it and read it to me"—and listening to it, Raskolnikov asserts that if he reveals his crime to her the following day, "I'm not coming to you to *ask* forgiveness, but simply to *tell* you" [italics mine]. The consistently self-righteous and adamant tone of his previous assertions lends a special significance to Raskolnikov's act of asking Sonia for her New Testament. The nature of the will as a kind of "voice"—commanding or asking, proclaiming or receiving, murdering or seeking forgiveness—is crucial to the nature of the word one speaks, hears, and obeys. For Raskolnikov in his proud and isolated will, the word is severed from any deeper faith or moral law and therefore must—as he freely admits even before his conversion—ultimately destroy. For Raskolnikov after his conversion and in the mystery of his newly moved, more submissive and receptive will, the Word may finally redeem.

What's So Funny About *Crime and Punishment*?

R.L. Busch

Although *Crime and Punishment* is not a comic novel, it contains several humorous passages. R.L. Busch, professor of Slavic and East European studies at the University of Alberta in Edmonton (Canada), examines these scenes carefully and discusses the ways in which Dostoyevsky uses them to subtly color his depiction of certain characters in the novel. Busch argues that Dostoyevsky's use of humor creates the irony necessary for the author to discredit the ideas or behaviors of characters like Marmeladov or Lebezyatnikov: The comic, often parodic, ways in which Dostoyevsky presents these characters makes it difficult, or impossible, to take them or their ideas seriously.

The first of Dostoevsky's five major novels is marked by extensive tonal counterpoint. Petersburg's stifling slums provide the physical backdrop for various crimes, including murder, which is focused on with clinical precision in respect to the act itself and, especially, in respect to the experience of the murderer, Rodion Raskolnikov, whose agony after the act dominates most of the novel. Tonal counterpoint to this grim subject matter is provided largely by black humor and by "reduced laughter"—especially by irony.

In depicting Raskolnikov, Dostoevsky resumes his strong opposition to radical-progressive and nihilist currents which had surfaced most saliently in *Notes from Underground* (1864). In Raskolnikov Dostoevsky portrays a young man of great intelligence and boldness who can find partial justification for murder in the radical ideas of the early 1860s. His intended victim, Alyona Ivanovna, is a wicked, religiously bigoted old pawnbroker who epitomizes the para-

Excerpted from R.L. Busch, *Humor in the Major Novels of F.M. Dostoevsky* (Columbus, OH: Slavica, 1987). Copyright ©1987 by Robert L. Busch. Reprinted with permission.

sitic socio-economic relationships which enable the haves to bleed the have-nots. Add strong atheistic inclinations, a mathematical approach to ethics, which excuses a lesser crime if it can facilitate many good deeds, and further, a theory that allows some enlightened and exceptional *progressive* individuals to step across (perestupit') conventional ethical norms, and one gets a [summary] of that complex of *new* ideas which could help Raskolnikov to rationalize murder.

Dostoevsky suspected that such ideas might well be a smokescreen for misanthropes who, in the name of humanity, seek to impose their own will on others. The novel's narrator is, with rarest exception, dispassionate and non-judgmental, so opposition to Raskolnikov, the criminal, comes from: his own nature, which so torments him as a result of the crime that it makes his ideas appear folly; from important "idea-bearing" characters (Sonya Marmeladova, Porfiry Petrovich, Razumikhin); and also, quite significantly, from the irony to which he is subject.

Irony is a reduced form of laughter, which is aggressive in nature and generally painful for the one against whom it is directed. It is especially typical of the "extremely reduced laughter" of *Crime and Punishment.* In treating humor in this work, it is important to give particular attention to irony, including that which is generated by Raskolnikov's parodic satellite figures—Lebezyatnikov, Luzhin, Svidrigailov. Additionally, one can point to Dostoevsky's exploiting contrastive effects involving the horrific and the buffoonish, the tragic and the comic.

In *Crime and Punishment,* Dostoevsky usually manages to include humorous elements in even the most harrowing or pathetic of scenes. Often noted has been the episode involving Raskolnikov's first meeting with Marmeladov. As George Gibian aptly noted, the novel's very important theme of suffering is introduced on a nearly burlesque level. Marmeladov, whose name is as silly as it sounds, is simultaneously both pathetic and comic. His own situation is hopeless, his story tragic. However, the style of his discourse lends dissonant comic notes to his tale of woe. This stems in part from his use of highfalutin utterance as in the following:

> And all during that *heavenly day of my life* and all during that evening I myself *whiled away* the hours in *soaring dreams*; that is to say I was thinking how I would arrange everything, clothe the *kiddies*, give her *tranquility*, and return *my daughter, my only born*, to the *bosom of the family.* (emphasis added)

A comic incongruity results from Dostoevsky's countering both the "lowdown" figure of the besotted Marmeladov and his unseemly story of Sonya's being sold into prostitution with rhetorical flourishes similar to those we have highlighted. Marmeladov's soliloquy is further infused with a comic tone through its combining Church-Slavic [an earlier form of Russian, whose use in the nineteenth century would be roughly as odd as Herman Melville's using Shakespearian English] or archaic elements such as *dscher'* (daughter), *priidi* (come*) grexi tvoi mnozi* (thy many sins) with *cute* diminutives such as *p'ianen'kii* (drunk), *slaben'kii* (weak), etc. Still further in this regard one can refer to rhetorical flourishes being countered by lapses in logic attributable to Marmeladov's inebriated condition:

> When my only born daughter started her yellow card [a prostitute's registration document] for the first time and then I too started.

> Do you know, good sir, do you know that I even drank her stockings? Not her shoes, sir, for that would at least be in the order of things, but her stockings, I drank her stockings, sir.

The inherent humor of Marmeladov's soliloquy is brought out not only through its style, but by the guffaws and jeers of the pothouse owner and a number of the patrons. Even after Marmeladov's protestation that, unlike the wise and calculating, the All-merciful will forgive not only his self-sacrificing daughter, but him and his ilk as well, his tirade is met with a similar response:

> His words produced a certain effect; for a minute silence reigned, but soon the former laughter and curses broke out:

> "The prophet has spoken!"

> "Rubbish!"

> "A fine civil servant!"

This reaction is later paralleled by that of Marmeladov's co-dwellers, who crowd around to be entertained by the spectacle of Katerina Ivanovna beating her wayward husband. Furthermore, but in a quite different vein, Marmeladov adds his own note of depraved laughter following his admission that he was not just a helpless and unwilling accessory to Sonya's becoming a prostitute, but that he turned to her for money to continue his drinking:

> But today I went to Sonya's to ask her for sobering-up money! Ha, ha, ha!

The response to Marmeladov here is typical, not just for the episode in question, but for the novel:

> "Did she really give it to you?" shouted one of the newcomers, who then began laughing for all he was worth.

Besides providing typical counterpoint to the pathos connected with Marmeladov and his family situation, the laughter here also serves to ridicule the baseness of Marmeladov's actions. This is a traditional function for the comic. At the same time the ridiculousness of the situation reinforces in Raskolnikov, the would-be rebel, a sense of the absurdity of the world, and, therefore, it can help convince him of the correctness of his superman theory and its formula for change. This is clear from the concluding paragraph to the chapter under discussion. Having derided the Marmeladovs for their exploitation of Sonya, and having concluded that man in his baseness can put up with anything, Raskolnikov adds:

> "But what if I'm talking nonsense," he exclaimed suddenly and involuntarily. "What if man is not really a *scoundrel*, not completely, no in general, all mankind that is [i.e., what if there are some great men, me for instance] then all the rest is just so much prejudice and self-imposed fear, and there are no barriers, and so it should come to pass (tomu i sleduet byt')."

THE COMIC AND THE TRAGIC ARE NEVER PURE IN DOSTOEVSKY

The foregoing use of counterpoint can serve to substantiate Donald Fanger's contention that neither comedy nor tragedy (and we could add here the pathetic) are ever pure in Dostoevsky. Certainly not in *Crime and Punishment*. Raskolnikov's portentous nightmare in which Mikolka and others beat to death the scrawny old roan offers further evidence of this. The scene combines: the horrific and the gruesome, i.e., the merciless killing of the roan; the pathetic, underscored by the reaction of Raskolnikov the child; the comic, expressed through the reaction of a number of the bystanders and participants in the killing; and also, something tangential to the comic, the grotesque, in the sense of the ludicrous and bizarre. These are evident in the expectation that the aged, rundown nag will not only pull the enormous weight of the cart, but will break into a gallop. They are also heightened by the fat, ruddy woman, who climbs aboard the cart laughing and eating nuts. The carnivalesque revelry of the crowd serves to underscore the insensitivity and cruelty of the world. In this regard the incident, which is so vividly recalled by Raskolnikov and which for the moment causes him to recoil in horror at the prospect of murder, may be seen as having contributed to his rebelliousness.

On the morning immediately after Raskolnikov murders the pawnbroker and her sister, he is summoned to the police station where he goes fearing the worst and already sorely beset by the need to confess. The scene at the police station features Raskolnikov's dread, but it is also rich in humorous counterpoint. Complementing Raskolnikov's innermost motives for fear at this juncture is the brazen and fiery police lieutenant, Ilya Petrovich, who takes an immediate dislike to Raskolnikov. Ilya Petrovich is the first to express suspicion of him in connection with the murder of Alyona Ivanovna. At the same time, in the fearsome lieutenant's swagger and overall short-fused demeanor there is something ludicrous. His remarks to Raskolnikov here are full of sarcasm. To Raskolnikov, a ragged student who has had the audacity to insist that he show some civility, Ilya Petrovich remarks:

> Complaints against you. You're not paying up. Ah, what a fine specimen you are!

And when Raskolnikov waxes loquacious in expressing surprise that his I.O.U. had been turned over by his landlady to the authorities:

> "All these sentimental details do not concern us, my dear sir," interrupted Ilya Petrovich brazenly. "You have to make a declaration and a promise, and as for how you deigned to fall in love together with all the tragic parts, well that matters not a jot to us."

Of course, Ilya Petrovich's malevolent sarcasm is potentially threatening to Raskolnikov, so his remarks, although meant to ridicule and to be perceived as humorous, are at the same time sinister and painful for Raskolnikov. Something closer to pure comic relief within this scene is provided by the flouncy *beperfumed* lady's answer to Ilya Petrovich's charges of running a house of ill repute. The altercation between Ilya Petrovich and her provides Raskolnikov with great pleasure, so much so that he feels the urge to break out in peals of laughter. And well he might. The content of her story aside, the flouncy lady's Germanized Russian is hilarious—as one can gather from the following short excerpt from her spiel:

> Und dey come completely drunk, und den dey ask again tree pottles, und den one raised a leg und starts wit das legs dee piano zu play, und dees not nice in nople house, und he break

> dee ganz piano. . . . Und dees is not a nople guest, mister Kap-
> itan, und he was always shkandal making! 'I', he says, 'will a
> peeg satire on you drucken, pecause I can write in all dee
> peeg newspaper'.

The last remark suggests to Ilya Petrovich that the villain of
the narrative was a member of the writing set, vagrants all,
a judgement he supports with a few choice anecdotes. As already noted, even Raskolnikov finds the flouncy lady up-
roarious. His desire to burst out in *genuine* peals of laughter
here is unique to the novel. His momentary mirth serves to
emphasize the grim state of terrified isolation into which he
is about to pass. The foregoing farcical interval is located between two stages in the novel, where Raskolnikov, the subjective focal point for the reader's perceptions, is horror
struck, i.e., the call to the police station delivered by the janitor whose axe was *borrowed* for the murder, and his faint-
ing followed by the insinuations of Ilya Petrovich that he is
suspected of the murders which were just being discussed.
Such is the humorous shading that Dostoevsky uses to take
his reader on an emotional roller-coaster ride during which
the sensation of peril predominates.

Part Two of the novel, one of almost constant physical and
mental crisis for Raskolnikov, is marked by numerous [in-
stances of comic contrast]. The vehicle for many of these is the
effervescent Razumikhin, whose material fortunes, on the
one hand, and whose nature, on the other, so significantly co-
incide and contrast with those of Raskolnikov. Thus Razumikhin's account of the publishing *shenanigans* of one Kheru-
vimov contrasts with Raskolnikov's delirium and sense of
acute alienation. And whether Razumikhin be teasing the
maid, Nastasya, punningly mocking the gibberish of the messenger who comes to deliver twenty-five rubles from Raskolnikov's mother, boasting of his bountiful affair with Pashenka,
Raskolnikov's landlady, or expounding on the virtues of the
second-hand clothes he has purchased for Raskolnikov, all
his banter is perceived in contrast to a sick, alienated and terrified Raskolnikov. Furthermore, as his name suggests, Razumikhin's lively speech contains either a knowledge of or a sinister suggestion of much that Raskolnikov fears revealing. As
examples one can cite his contention that he knows all about
Raskolnikov. "I, my friend, have found out all there is to know
about you." Consider also his response to Raskolnikov's concern about what he had said while delirious:

> Ugh, how you do go on! Might you not fear for some sort of
> secret? Don't worry, you didn't talk about the countess. But
> you did say a heap about some bulldog or other, yes, and
> about earrings, and oh yes, about some little chains, and also
> about Krestov Island, and also about some janitor or other,
> and also about Ilya Petrovich, the Assistant to the Police In-
> spector. And, oh yes, in addition, you even were pleased to be
> interested in your little old sock. Very much so indeed. You
> kept crying out: 'Give it here.' Zamyotov himself searched all
> over the place for your sock. With his daintily washed, beper-
> fumed and bejeweled hands, he scrounged around just so's
> he could give you that crap.

And Raskolnikov is not to fret? The only thing he failed to do
in his delirium was to own up to everything in Zamyotov's
presence, something he will all but do during the game of
cat and mouse he plays with him at the Crystal Palace. Razumikhin's jocular tone is once again double-edged when he
adduces the reasons for Mikolai's and Mitrey's innocence
while using their own substandard, comically deformed
speech, as well as that of the barkeep Dushkin. From this
Razumikhin proceeds to an accurate account of Raskolnikov's escape from the scene of the crime. It is for this reason that by the time Dunya's suitor, Luzhin, arrives on the
scene, Raskolnikov is said to resemble a man who has just
undergone a painful operation or emerged from a torture
chamber. In bringing him to this state Dostoevsky has made
liberal use of intrinsically comic touches to point up his protagonist's terror.

Torn between life and death, i.e., the need to confess, on the
one hand, and the need to commit suicide, on the other,
Raskolnikov sneaks out following his altercation with Luzhin.
Two brushes with death, or with near death, Afrosinyushka's
attempted suicide and Marmeladov's fatal accident, turn
Raskolnikov away from suicide. His need to confess is
brought out in his mock confession to Zamyotov at the Crystal Palace. It is further underlined by his resolve to go to the
police station after Afrosinyushka's attempt to drown herself,
and by his trying to get suspicious bystanders to take him to
the police following his return to the scene of the crime. Here,
Dostoevsky interlards Raskolnikov's re-experiencing gory details of the crime and his compromising statements and actions with the comic parlance of the decorators:

> The older one was saying to the younger: "Well don't you
> know, she comes to me in the wee early hours of the morn-
> ing, and she's all decked out, see. And why for, I says, are you

all dolled up that way, why for, are you all gussied up like that? And she says to me: 'From here on out and in the future, Tit Vasilich, I want for all of me to be under your command.' So that's the way it is! And was she ever dolled up. Just like a magazine she was, a real magazine!"

[. . .] In addition to the comic relief provided by the painters' exchange, Dostoevsky also manages to work in here one of many *polyphonic* reverberations with Raskolnikov's superman theory which construably contributed to his committing murder. "From here on out and in the future, Tit Vasilich, I want for all of me to be under your command," is a variation on Raskolnikov's division of people into a super elite to whom all is permitted and the others over whom they exercise their will. To be sure, in the case of Tit Vasilich and his gal, the power to rule appears to be freely given, but their roles fit the Raskolnikov division of mankind into ruler and ruled, and therefore provide a comic echo with his theory.

COMIC ELEMENTS OF THE MARMELADOV WOMEN AND PORFIRY

Further on in Part Two, the scene of Marmeladov on his deathbed is also nuanced with comic elements in Katerina Ivanovna's quarrel with her landlady whose bastardized Russian parallels that of the flouncy lady at the police station. The stylistic coloration apart, their argument is ludicrous because of Katerina Ivanovna's prideful pretentiousness, which causes her to represent Raskolnikov as an august benefactor with connections. The comic aspect is further brought out here by the narrator's acknowledging the laughter outside the door accompanied by the shout: "They're having at it!" As with the circus-like atmosphere that accompanied the beating of the horse in Part One, the laughter here serves to emphasize man's cruelty and capacity for insensitivity to the plight of others.

Shortly following Katerina Ivanovna's quarrel with her landlady, Sonya appears in the outlandish dress of her profession. This marks one of the outstanding examples of the grotesque in the novel:

> . . . her attire was cheap but street-gaudy. Loudly and shamefully bespeaking its objective, it was in conformity with the taste and rules of its own particular world. Sonya stood in the entryway right at the doorstep which she did not cross. She looked confused and unaware of anything. Forgotten was her colorful, fourth-hand silk dress, which was out of place here with its extravagantly long and ridiculous train and an enor-

mous hoop-skirt that blocked the whole doorway, forgotten were her bright shoes and her parasol, which was superfluous at night, forgotten too, her silly straw hat with its flaming red feather. Out from beneath the hat, which was cocked at a childish angle, there looked a thin, pale and frightened little face, its mouth open and its eyes transfixed by fear.

Although Sonya's dress is inherently ludicrous, any amused reaction is undercut by Marmeladov's horror at being confronted during his last moments with the corrupting effect of his own weakness on his daughter.

Far more plentiful in tragic and comic elements, including the farcical, is the scandalous funeral dinner for Marmeladov. Katerina Ivanovna, showing signs of madness and imminent death from tuberculosis, seeks pathetically to assert her nobility before a rag-tag crowd of guests. Among others, these include a drunk and disorderly supply officer, a tongue-tied, and *zit-faced* civil servant, a deaf and nearly blind old man, and a scrawny Pole who brought along a couple of compatriots whom nobody had ever seen before. This motley crew, together with Raskolnikov, Katerina Ivanovna's family and her German landlady, provides a suitably bizarre mixture for one of Dostoevsky's patented *scandal scenes*. These are consistently characterized by both high emotional tension and a laughable break in decorum.

Katerina Ivanovna's derisive mockery of her guests, including her arch-enemy, Amalya Ivanovna, is perceived against the background of both a solemn religious ritual and her own desperate condition. The scene builds up to a chaotic break in decorum following Luzhin's abortive attempt to compromise Sonya. The playoff of tragic and comic elements can be subsumed by Katerina Ivanovna's own laughter which is repeatedly broken by coughing spasms (Kha-kha-kha! kkhi-kkhi-kkhi!). Once again, however, the tragic note predominates, for the disgracing of Luzhin notwithstanding, the dying Katerina Ivanovna and her family have been ordered out onto the street with nowhere to go and Sonya, offended, despairing and hysterical, has been made to confront as never before the seemingly irredeemable evil in the world.

Further striking examples of the playoff of humor and terror can be found in the duels involving the criminal investigator, Porfiry Petrovich, and Raskolnikov. The counterpoint appears at the outset of the very first encounter between the two antagonists. At this meeting, which Raskolnikov has so much to fear, he shows up fairly bursting with laughter. Incongruously, it is Razumikhin who, having been teased over his attraction to Dunya, takes on the violent demeanor of a hounded person. The narrator informs the reader that Razumikhin's enraged reaction to Raskolnikov's taunting imparted to their entry the appearance of "the most sincere gaiety, and, what is most important, nonchalance." The banter between the two continues, but a chilling ingredient is suddenly introduced by the unexpected presence of Zamyotov to whom Raskolnikov had all but confessed the night before.

Porfiry Petrovich, a figure who both in terms of plot suspense and theme (suffering and redemption), is central to the novel, *embodies* the pervasive mixture of humor and terror in the work. The physical description of Porfiry suggests as much. His rotund corpulence and beardlessness are laughable—as he himself states: "God Himself arranged my shape so that it only arouses comic thoughts in others; I'm a buffoon, sir." Porfiry's alert and mocking countenance might be taken as a sign of his being good-natured were it not for the expression of the eyes, whose watery sheen, beneath white blinking lids, makes it seem as though he is winking at someone. Porfiry's contrastive aspect is underlined by the narrator:

> Somehow the look of those eyes strangely failed to harmonize with his overall appearance, which was even somewhat womanish; their gaze imparted to it a much more serious air than one could have expected at first glance.

Raskolnikov will forthwith encounter both an apparent knowing wink and Porfiry's mocking tone in response to his devious question about the type of paper suitable for informing Porfiry of the personal items he had left with Alyona Ivanovna:

> "Oh, on the very simplest, sir!"—and suddenly Porfiry looked at him with openly mocking eyes; he squinted and seemed to wink knowingly . . .

> With lightening speed it flashed through Raskolnikov's mind: "He knows!"

Although Porfiry's comic side comes out in all three of the tense scenes involving him and Raskolnikov, the counterpoint reaches its peak during their second meeting. Raskolnikov quakes from fear and feels a boundless hatred for Porfiry both prior to and during their confrontation. Almost throughout this scene, Porfiry's comic aspect is brought out by: his familiar tone, e.g., "my good sir" (pochtenneishii), "old chap" (batiushka); his cute diminutives, e.g., "lil' divan" (divanchik), "lil' example" (primerchik), "lil' expression" (vyrazhen'itse), "lil' surprise" (siurprizik), etc.; his nearly incessant "motion" (motsion) about the room, during which his round, pudgy figure is compared to a ball bouncing from wall to wall—a movement sinisterly broken by Porfiry's sudden halts to stare right into Raskolnikov's face; his incessant laughter and his steady stream of "senseless rambling chatter"/pustaia sbivchivaia boltovnia. All of these impart to Porfiry a clownishness, which is nevertheless counterbalanced by his clever and sinister insinuations which drive Raskolnikov into an uncontrollable rage. It is clear that by the end of the chapter, Porfiry has readied his prey for the *coup de grace*, the *siurprizik* waiting outside. However, this time the joke is on Porfiry. Mikolka unexpectedly confesses to murdering Alyona Ivanovna, so Raskolnikov goes free.

WHY DOSTOEVSKY USES COMEDY

We have certainly not exhausted the intermixing and juxtaposition of tragic and intrinsically comic elements in the novel, nor could we hope to. However, their interplay has been sufficiently indicated. What is the function of this interplay? A single all-encompassing answer could not be adequate. The just-referred to joke on Porfiry serves an immediate plot function, i.e., a sharp, unexpected reversal in Raskolnikov's situation. Porfiry's joking in the scene serves potentially as a counterweight to the agony to which Raskolnikov is subject. However, at the same time, Porfiry's devious jesting also contributes to Raskolnikov's agony. Here, the function or effect of the interplay is relative, depending upon the degree of a given reader's detachment from or empathy with Raskolnikov. Something approaching pure comic relief is discernible in the person of the flouncy lady at the police station. A potentially dual function in Dostoevsky's use of buffoonish clownishness and drollery is asserted by N.M. Chirkov. He sees these as occasionally undermining pathos through parody. However, he argues, their main effect is to heighten pathos.

In view of the dissonant tonality that abounds in the novel, Raskolnikov himself is not a *purely* tragic figure. He is lowered through irony and through his parodic counterparts, Luzhin, Lebezyatnikov and Svidrigailov. Irony regularly serves as a macabre form of humor within *Crime and Punishment* where it is encountered very frequently. An outstanding example might be Porfiry's *surprise* when Mikolka confesses. Indeed, one could extensively develop the subject of irony with respect only to belief or non-belief in Raskolnikov's guilt as manifested by Porfiry, Razumikhin, Dunya, Pulkheriya Ivanovna, Zamyotov, Ilya Petrovich, and the burgher. However, we will concentrate on irony as it affects Raskolnikov. In so doing, we will pay particular attention both to information about him and to his actions and statements, which, as a result of misguided expectations, prove to be ironic and thereby tend to lower him. Here one confronts an important principle involving the tragic. In order to preserve the integrity of a tragic character, it appears essential that the character not be a direct party to buffoonery, or to that which renders him ridiculous. Furthermore, the narrator cannot . . . make fun of his protagonist without lowering him from the tragic pedestal he might otherwise occupy.

There is a wealth of irony surrounding Raskolnikov's preparation for and commission of the crime. Just as will be the case with Raskolnikov's parodic satellites, most of the irony involving his preparation for and commission of the crime will tend to point up the inadequacy of reason and egotistical calculation—or, at least, Raskolnikov's reasoning and calculation.

Much of Part One of the novel involves Raskolnikov's ambivalence with respect to the murder he is contemplating. The immediately decisive factor in his resolve to go ahead with the crime is his learning that Alyona Ivanovna is to be alone at 7:00 p.m. on the following evening. Instead of capitalizing on this, Raskolnikov oversleeps and reaches her apartment at 7:30. The oversleeping is the first of a series of practical mistakes that show this proudly calculating man to be a blunderer. This initial blunder is crucial, because it will lead to his encounter with the *holy* Lizaveta, whose murder will significantly alter the *moral equation* underlying the crime.

The reader is informed by a tongue-in-cheek narrator that Raskolnikov had not been given to think through the minute details concerning the execution of the murder. He was sure that these would be taken care of just by maintaining his will power and reason. It is not these, however, but mere happenstance that will pull the novice through. Consequently, a janitor's absence and a protruding axe save the day, when an utterly disoriented, enraged and weaponless Raskolnikov discovers that Nastasya is in the kitchen, thereby making her axe unavailable, which was hardly a brilliant choice to begin with. Raskolnikov's ironic smile and remark, "If not by my wit, then by the devil" are indicative of the insufficiency of his reason. His failure to carry out his intention of exchanging his glaringly noticeable top hat for something more in keeping with his ragged dress is another example of the failure of Raskolnikov, the calculator.

However, immediately prior to the crime itself, it is the narrator's caustic remarks on Raskolnikov's cerebrations concerning crime and its attendant symptoms which are bearers of the greatest irony. Raskolnikov has concluded that, while committing a crime, almost every criminal is subject to a loss of will and reason which are replaced at the most inopportune time by a phenomenally childish light-headedness. He further knows that crimes are preceded, accompanied, and followed by illness. However, the question as to whether the illness is the cause or the result of the crime, was something he was incapable of resolving. But then it mattered little, for he felt himself to be immune from any such symptoms:

> Having reached such conclusions, Raskolnikov decided that, in his case, there could be no such pathological turnabouts, that he would totally maintain his will and intellect while carrying out his plan—the reason for this being that what he had planned was "not a crime."

However, Raskolnikov's actions and state of mind belie his sophistry. For he has unwittingly fallen into the very state he has described as typical of the common criminal. This is well illustrated by his light-headed thoughts on the way to Alyona Ivanovna's:

> At that time he was preoccupied with irrelevant thoughts which came and went rapidly. On his way past the Yusupov Gardens he started getting quite engrossed with the way high-spouting fountains are built and how nicely they might freshen the air on all the squares. Gradually, he arrived at the conviction that if one were to extend the Summer Gardens all the way through the Martian Fields, and even connect them to the Mikhailovsky Palatial Gardens, it would be a wonderful and highly practical thing for the city. Then he was suddenly taken with considering why it was that in all large cities men were inclined not by necessity, but by some other special reason, to settle not amidst gardens or fountains, but amidst filth, stench and every other sort of rot . . . for a mo-

ment he came to. "What nonsense," he thought. "No, it's better not to think at all!"

Clearly, Raskolnikov has lost control and is ironically remote from the self-image he nourishes. It is further ironic that in this instance, as in many others, he is aware of his weakness before the fact, but will not, or cannot, heed the warnings.

Further on, as Raskolnikov stands before the door of his victim, this haughty intellect and would-be superman is barely conscious of his body, and his mind is going blank.

Once he has murdered the old pawnbroker, Raskolnikov increasingly loses control. Having convinced himself that she was dead, he stops his pilfering to go back and kill her all over again. Reassured that she really is dead, he engages in a two-minute struggle with the cord around her neck. He considers hacking it off with the axe, then comes to the more reasonable conclusion that it had best be cut off. But with the axe rather than with his clasp knife! His drawn out fumbling with the keys and his rummaging through his victim's trunks are further examples of his loss of self-control. As will be noted later by Razumikhin, the novice knew only how to kill. This he does forthrightly enough to the terrified Lizaveta who totally surprises him because he has all the while left the apartment door open. Following this second murder, Raskolnikov is once again overcome by distractedness to such a degree that he again forgets to close the door. And when he does, he only fastens it with a hook rather than lock it with the key that is in it. Thus, the image of Raskolnikov, the *transgressor* (perestupaiushchii), is essentially that of a mindless blunderer and ordinary mortal for whom the laws of nature prohibit calculated bloodshed. Just as he had ironically suspected well before the fact, a Napoleon or one of mankind's elite he is not, so only extremely fortuitous circumstances allow him to escape temporarily to a life of terror and alienation that often rivals the chilling effects of the murder scene at the end of Part One.

THE COMIC TREATMENT OF THE AFTERMATH OF THE CRIME

Raskolnikov is the subject of significant irony on a number of occasions after the crime. Already in Part Two it is deeply ironic that the equally impecunious Razumikhin can so quickly exploit the very situation in which Raskolnikov had been living. Clean linen, a splendid table setting, excellent food, the return of the I.O.U. from Chebarov, the intimate favors of Raskolnikov's landlady, Pashenka, all this Razumikhin achieves overnight. Such irony serves not only to lower Raskolnikov, but also to undermine the sociological factors which might have seemed sufficient cause for his committing the crime.

At the end of Part Two Raskolnikov is fortuitously *saved* from confessing his crime when he chances upon the scene of an accident in which Marmeladov has been fatally injured. Following this second brush with death in the course of a few hours, Raskolnikov returns to the scene of the first, namely the bridge from which Afrosinyushka jumped in her attempt to commit suicide. Here Raskolnikov expresses his resolve to fight on:

> "Enough!" he declared decisively and triumphantly. "Away with the mirages and imaginary fears, away with phantoms! There's life to be lived. Was I not living just now? My life has not died with the old biddy! Heaven bless her soul, and well that's that, old girl, it's time for you to rest! Now there'll be the kingdom of reason and light and . . . and will, and power . . . and well now we'll just see," he added feistily, as though turning to and calling forth some dark force.

Raskolnikov clearly believes his illness to have passed and expresses the conviction that nothing is obtainable without power, while power itself is only attainable through power. So go his thoughts, while physically he is barely able to set one foot in front of the other! Furthermore, Raskolnikov has drastically compromised himself both by his remarks to Zamyotov and by his suspicious return to the scene of the crime. The narrator intimates that Raskolnikov is being a bit hasty here, and indeed, the end of the scene will prove it. For as he approaches his lodging, after having ascertained from Razumikhin's drunken spiel that the authorities do suspect him, and that Zamyotov has told, in the presence of Porfiry, all about the near confession at the Crystal Palace, Raskolnikov believes the light in his room to indicate that he is to be arrested. Petrified and resigned to the inevitable, he faints as Part Two concludes. In view of this, Raskolnikov's proud utterances on power and his vow to match strength with his adversaries are extremely ironic.

Further on, it is Porfiry, not the isolated Raskolnikov, who has knowledge of the publication of Raskolnikov's own article, "On Crime." Even Raskolnikov's mother sees it in print before its author. Her remarks concerning the article, which reveal the great pride she takes in her son, are painfully ironic in view of Raskolnikov's imminent plans to go off to prison:

> "I read it, my dear, and, of course, there's a lot I don't understand; but that's to be expected, for how am I to keep up with you? . . .

> "Only, Rodya dear, I may be dense, but still I can see that you will soon be one of the foremost, and maybe even the foremost man in our scholarly world. And they dared to think that you had gone mad. Ha, ha, ha! You don't know it, but that's what they were thinking."

Closely relatable in function to irony are the parodic figures of Lebezyatnikov, Luzhin and Svidrigailov. Significant characterological parallels exist between them and Raskolnikov. These parallels allow them, at various levels of seriousness, to mimic Raskolnikov and thereby lower both him and what he represents.

The most comic of the three is the scrofular, weakbrained Lebezyatnikov through whom Dostoevsky ridicules Russia's radical progressives and, especially, their vulgarizers. Like Raskolnikov, Lebezyatnikov stands for a sharp break with the past, but both are subverted in this by their own natures and by the weight of tradition. To Lebezyatnikov Marmeladov attributed the credo that compassion is outlawed by science. Lebezyatnikov confirms this general notion in a later exchange with Luzhin. Nevertheless, he, like Raskolnikov, displays ambivalence in this regard. Thus, he admits to being favorably impressed by Luzhin's act of charity on behalf of the Marmeladov family. Furthermore, he too will show compassion when Katerina Ivanovna, with fatal consequences, takes to the streets with her children. Such acts of compassion are paralleled by Raskolnikov. One side of his dual nature manifests concern for his fellow man—his intercession on behalf of the drunk and molested girl, his aid to the Marmeladovs, his professed concern for humanity, etc. Both he and Lebezyatnikov profess to see in Sonya a symbol of human suffering and social injustice and, accordingly, they express their respect for her. Nevertheless, both he and Lebezyatnikov stand for an attachment to one's own properly understood self-interest, the *dada* of N.G. Chernyshevsky and his fellow radical progressives. The resultant *outlawing* of compassion manifests itself in a murderous form in Raskolnikov, in a milder form in Lebezyatnikov.

With respect to Raskolnikov, little discoursing on the subject is needed. One should stress, however, that he steadfastly refuses to consider the murder of the innocent Lizaveta, who can be seen as a symbol of suffering, downtrodden humanity. As for Lebezyatnikov, a lack of compassion is apparent in his beating of Katerina Ivanovna and in his insistence that Sonya vacate the tenement house when her family's need drives her into prostitution. Here the force of prejudice and, more importantly, Lebezyatnikov's own nature, interfere with his strictly rational beliefs. He had been seeking Sonya's affections, so it is clear that his *amourpropre* has been affected:

> "It's because of Sonya that the incident with Katerina Ivanovna took place. At first he himself was trying to get at Sonya, so his ego was bruised: 'How am I, such an educated man, supposed to live in the same flat with such a slut?'"

In a similar way, a traditional ethical imperative will cry out in Lebezyatnikov when he catches Luzhin falsely accusing Sonya of robbery. Luzhin is only applying the principle of calculated self-interest, but Lebezyatnikov recoils before it. In a like way, albeit on a different level, Raskolnikov's nature recoiled before his application of the same theory.

A further significant feature held in common by Raskolnikov and Lebezyatnikov is their approach to theoretical models. Lebezyatnikov is irritated at Luzhin's reservations concerning the new ethical standards of the projected communal society—wives and children in common, universal latrine-cleaning duties, etc. He insists that neophytes must accept the whole system first before they get involved in the details. Such was Raskolnikov's approach to murder.

Finally, apropos of Katerina Ivanovna's deranged state, the ever *westernizing* Lebezyatnikov paraphrases a French authority and unwittingly identifies a significant facet of Raskolnikov's own problem—namely, that madness results from "a mistake in logic, an error in judgement, the wrong outlook on things." All of these fit Raskolnikov to the letter. Viewed in terms of the characterological hierarchy of the novel, a ludicrous situation emerges. As the Russian proverb might put it, the egg is teaching the hen. Although Lebezyatnikov is the least developed of the three parodic satellites, a caricature of Russia's nihilistic radicals, his parodic function is not at all diminished thereby. Indeed, one can argue the converse.

LUZHIN AND SVIDRIGAILOV AS FOILS FOR RASKOLNIKOV

A less clownish, more sinister parody figure for Raskolnikov is Luzhin. Dostoevsky reinforces certain ideational and behavioral links between the two by having them both appear in new outfits when they first meet—Luzhin's fresh from the tailor, Raskolnikov's from the second-hand shop. Luzhin, a pompously self-important schemer, is extensively associated with a belief in calculating self-interest. This self-interest dominates his projected marriage to Raskolnikov's sister. His carefully made plans to set himself up as the benefactor of the impoverished Raskolnikovs go awry, so the inadequacy of reason alone is illustrated. Additionally, it is implied that not only Luzhin but Raskolnikov too has played a calculating game in affairs of the heart. In explaining to Ilya Petrovich and Nikodim Fomich the I.O.U. turned over by his landlady, Raskolnikov argues that, in return for credit, he gave only a non-binding, verbal promise to marry her sickly daughter whom he claims not to have loved.

Like Raskolnikov, Luzhin expresses a belief in power. This alone he fears and is ready to respect in the Progressives. Are they in power? Might they expose him? This is what he wants to ascertain from Lebezyatnikov. Reason and *enlightened* self-interest occasion both Raskolnikov and Luzhin to commit crimes—the unsuccessful attempt to defame Sonya in the case of the latter. Thus, on a lower level is expressed the folly of principles which Chernyshevsky and his radical progressive followers had made into a fetish. Indeed, Raskolnikov emphasizes enlightened self-interest as a principle underlying his crime when he indignantly remarks to Luzhin: "So what are you fussing about? . . . It [the crime] was the result of your own theory."

Whereas Lebezyatnikov and Luzhin are lesser lights who parody some of Raskolnikov's ideas, it is somewhat different in the case of Svidrigailov. In his capacity for working evil, Svidrigailov is Raskolnikov's superior. Raskolnikov senses Svidrigailov's power over him as a result of the latter's apparent knowledge of his crime. Furthermore, the demonic Svidrigailov's power is given lofty symbolic overtones through his characterological and thematic juxtaposition to the Christian Sonya, and through the positioning of both him and Sonya during Raskolnikov's *confessional* sessions with her.

What is more, the links between Raskolnikov and Svidrigailov are more numerous than those between him and the other parodic figures. Both occasionally manifest demonic traits in their exterior physical features, their actions and their speech—e.g., their use in common of the phrase "assez causé," which links them to the Mephistophelean figure of Balzac's Vautrin. Both act sporadically and in differing degrees as benefactors to others. Both are fond of frequenting places of depravity and corruption. There are similarities in their tastes in women, Svidrigailov's depiction of his teenage fiancée revealing features in common with Sonya: more than beauty he prizes her childlike eyes, timidity and look of shame, and he is further attracted by her mournful expression of a holy fool in Christ. Both Svidrigailov and Raskolnikov are associated with murder. Both are beset by visions of their victims. Both are out contemplating suicide the night before Raskolnikov's confession. In sum, Dostoevsky supplies ample material to support Svidrigailov's contention that he and Raskolnikov are "berries from the same field"/odnogo polia iagody.

Like Raskolnikov's other satellite figures, Svidrigailov, too, is calculating and a believer in following his own self-interest. This is most apparent in his marriage to Marfa Petrovna, which was above all a business transaction. As was the case with Luzhin and Raskolnikov, an adherence to his own self-interest links Svidrigailov to crime. In his case, according to convincing circumstantial evidence, this has resulted in the death of several people, his most recent victim being Marfa Petrovna. Unlike Raskolnikov, however, Svidrigailov commits his crimes successfully. He eludes detection by the authorities and does not appear to suffer debilitating compunctions, although as stated, his victims do return to haunt him. Svidrigailov's relative *success* puts into relief Raskolnikov's failure.

The numerous features in common between Raskolnikov and Svidrigailov serve to bring home to Raskolnikov the vileness in his own behavior and character. With respect to parodic function, Svidrigailov serves as a grotesquely distorting mirror for many of their common features. This accounts for both Raskolnikov's extreme revulsion in the presence of Svidrigailov and Raskolnikov's eventual acceptance of Sonya's Christian solution.

Because he strikes Raskolnikov as morally hideous, because he knows about Raskolnikov's crime, and because he lusts after Dunya, Svidrigailov poses a serious threat to Raskolnikov. Thus he is more a source of dread than of humor. Nevertheless, the latter constitutes an important part of his characterization. Sarcasm pervades his speech. Both wittingly and unwittingly he parrots Raskolnikov's thoughts and utterances. Unwitting parroting is apparent at the very outset of their first meeting during which Svidrigailov so insists on their resemblance. Referring to his wooing of Dunya, he denies "criminal behavior." In stating his case he indirectly gives voice to a number of thoughts that have been besetting Raskolnikov:

> Therein lies the question: am I a tormentor, or *am I myself a victim?* After all, in proposing to the object of my attentions that we run off to America or Switzerland, maybe I was *harboring the most respectable sentiments, yes, and maybe I was trying to bring about our mutual happiness! After all, reason is the servant of passion!* Really, I was harming myself even more. (emphasis added)

Raskolnikov's immediate reaction to these words is one of revulsion, and this cannot be explained solely on the basis of what he has heard about Svidrigailov and his attentions to Dunya. Svidrigailov's words are eminently relatable to the nightmare Raskolnikov has just experienced and to the troubled thoughts that precede it. For Raskolnikov the question as to whether he was the tormentor or the victim is raised by the immediately ensuing punishing effects of his crime. The question has just been graphically put and answered in his nightmare, where Alyona Ivanovna mocks her frenzied attacker's futile attempts to kill her. It may indeed be argued that Raskolnikov did even more harm to himself than to Alyona Ivanovna. And, of course, his thoughts prior to the nightmare showed that he, too, had had pretensions of acting in the general welfare, and that his reason had been subservient to personal desires. Thus Svidrigailov's statements are marked by dramatic irony which is sensed by Raskolnikov.

In general, sarcasm or verbal irony is apparent in Svidrigailov's statements to or about Raskolnikov. Such statements *to* Raskolnikov are especially prominent in Part Six, Chapters Three-Five. In these chapters Svidrigailov, while recounting details of his depraved past, repeatedly taunts Raskolnikov for Schillerian scruples, which are so at odds with his crime:

> "It's not about that, no, not about that [Raskolnikov's confession to Sonya] (although I did hear something or other). No, I

am referring to your incessant ooing and ahing! The Schiller
in you is forever getting upset. So now one mustn't eavesdrop.
If that's the way it is, go and declare to the authorities that
such and such a thing happened-that there was just a teensy
weensy theoretical error. If you are convinced that one
shouldn't eavesdrop behind doors, but that one can bash little old ladies over the head with whatever comes to hand, and
as much as one wants, then get yourself off to America as fast
as you can."

This jesting at the expense of Raskolnikov's moral compunctions serves to underline both the difference and the
similarity between him and Svidrigailov.

With respect to verbal irony in utterances by Svidrigailov
about Raskolnikov, especially noteworthy is his summation
to Dunya of her brother's motives for committing his crime.
Svidrigailov expresses its theoretical basis as follows:

> Here he had his own little old theory—a so-so theory—accord-
> ing to which people are divided, you see, into material and into
> special people, that is, into people for whom, by dint of their
> lofty position, laws are not written, but who, rather, write laws
> for the other folks, i.e., for the material, that is, for the trash. Not
> bad, a so-so theory, une théorie comme une autre.

This exposition of Raskolnikov's theory stands in parodic
contrast to the one which was made during his first meeting
with Porfiry. Svidrigailov's overall recounting of Raskolnikov's motives likewise stands in parodic contrast to his
tormented confession to Sonya. Whereas statements like
those cited serve to lower Raskolnikov, the criminal and
would-be superman, Svidrigailov ultimately serves to raise
Raskolnikov from an ethical standpoint.

In a similar way, and yet to a greater degree than is true
of the other parodic satellites, Svidrigailov gives expression
to Dostoevsky's polyphonic technique in the novel. No *full-
throated* laughter results from the parodic doubling, for the
humor has a painful twist. The tonal counterpoint attendant
upon Svidrigailov's suicide is a case in point:

> A small sentry stood leaning against the large locked gates of
> the building. He was wrapped in a soldier's coat and wore a
> tiny helmet à la Achilles. With a drowsy glance he eyed the
> approaching Svidrigailov. On the sentry's face could be seen
> that eternal, peevish sorrow which has left such a dour im-
> print on every last one of the Jewish race. Both of them,
> Svidrigailov and Achilles, examined each other in silence for
> a while. At last Achilles deemed it unsuitable for a man who
> was not drunk to be staring silently at him from just three
> steps away.

"Vot you dooing here, eh?" he said, still not moving or altering his position.

"Why nothing, really. How're you doing, brother?"

"Dis place not for you."

"Hey brother, I'm off for distant lands."

"Distant lands?"

"To America."

"America?"

"Svidrigailov took out a revolver and cocked the hammer. Achilles raised his eyebrows.

"Dis place not for you. No choking around here." "What's wrong with this place?" "'Caus I'm telling you, dis place no good, no choking around here."

"Well brother, it makes no difference to me. The place is fine. If they should ask, you just tell them I went off to America."

Svidrigailov raised the revolver to his right temple.

"Heh! Vot you dooing? Dis place not dee place here," Achilles said, quivering, his pupils getting larger and larger.

Svidrigailov pulled the trigger.

Through his own comically lowered suicide, Svidrigailov underscores the ultimate bankruptcy of the calculating hedonism he embraced. This point is brought home to the reader, but not, for the time being, to Raskolnikov who must suffer the prison experience before accepting Sonya's way to rebirth.

Svidrigailov's dominant status among the parodic figures in the novel, as well as the predominance of sinister, threatening elements in his characterological function, would serve to substantiate Bakhtin's view on humor in Dostoevsky's mature fiction. The open laughter of the carnival tradition is replaced by a reduced form manifested in irony and other forms of humor. Nevertheless, *comic* elements, even if outweighed by *tragic* ones, constitute vital components in the first of Dostoevsky's five major novels.

CHAPTER 3

Raskolnikov on the Couch: Psychological Perspectives on *Crime and Punishment*

READINGS ON
CRIME AND PUNISHMENT

Dostoyevsky's Childhood and *Crime and Punishment*

Louis Breger

Many scholars have searched Dostoyevsky's lengthy notebooks for insight into the characters and events of *Crime and Punishment*. Louis Breger, professor of psychoanalytic studies at the California Institute of Technology, argues that Dostoyevsky has incorporated events from his own childhood into the novel. The names and depictions of certain characters, as well as entire scenes, are rooted in the psychologically troubling events of the author's youth.

Breger builds much of his argument in the following selection on an excerpt from Dostoyevsky's notebooks that recounts a childhood event that resembles the "horse-beating dream" Raskolnikov has early in the book. Breger argues that this small fragment of memory contains a number of the themes that Dostoyevsky develops in the novel. This article is, in many ways, very representative of the techniques that literary critics have borrowed and adapted from psychology.

A sound psychoanalytic interpretation of a dream rests on the dreamer's associations. Wouldn't it be nice if we could ask Dostoevsky himself for his associations to the many elements in *Crime and Punishment*? Where did he get the names for his characters, the repeated image of the cramped room with dirty yellow wallpaper, the idea of a self-destructive alcoholic husband (Marmeladov), the suffering horse? While we cannot ask him, we can treat the material that is available—*The Notebooks*, ideas expressed in his correspondence, information about his childhood, and recurring themes and images in the other novels—as if they all were associations.

. . . This analysis [of the novel] can be confirmed by bringing in these "associations," the surrounding material.

A central interpretation is that Dostoevsky expresses his conflicts toward women through a series of female pairs—the pawnbroker and Lizaveta, Raskolnikov's mother and Dunia, Katherine Marmeladov and Sonia, the landlady and her maid, Martha, and the young girls of Svidrigailov's dreams—who represent two sides of his ambivalence. One is the depriving, hated and the other the giving, loved mother figure. How do these characters link up with his own life? Katherine Marmeladov is modeled fairly directly on his first wife, Maria. She represents the angry-guilty connection with a sick and dying woman: Katherine's half-mad state in the final stages of her tuberculosis is drawn directly from Dostoevsky's observations of Maria. Since . . . the marriage was an unconscious reenactment of Dostoevsky's relation with the first Maria, his mother, this extends the link back into childhood.

There are additional associations along this path: Maria's first husband, the man she was with when Dostoevsky met her in Siberia, was an alcoholic who drank himself to death. Dostoevsky's own father turned to heavy drinking after his wife's death; drunkenness played a role in his murder by his serfs. In the article in which he recounts the horse and courier memory [see insert], Dostoevsky gives, as an example of the internalization of cruelty, the way beaten-down husbands turn to drink and abuse their wives and children. An early plan for *Crime and Punishment* was called *The Drunkards*; it was to have been an exposé of alcoholism. All these associative lines eventually found expression in the Marmeladov subplot of the novel. Marmeladov is the alcoholic who passes cruelty down the line, not by beating his wife, but with more complex masochistic aggression. . . .

MOTHERS AND SURROGATE MOTHERS

[Many characters'] names have more personal associations. I think it particularly significant that Dostoevsky gave the name Aliona to the old pawnbroker. While the deaths of several of the other women in the novel are brought about by indirect means, she is the object of a violent attack: she is the depriving, guilt-inducing mother figure in pure form. Why did this name come to him when he created her?

It was a name he knew well throughout his childhood:

Aliona Frolovna was the family nurse. She came to the Dos-
toevskys when Varvara, the sister born after Feodor, was an
infant, and was still on hand, caring for the youngest siblings, at the time of the father's death. Dostoevsky was originally nursed by a peasant woman whose name is unknown,
a wet nurse who was brought from the countryside for that

THE HORSE-COURIER MEMORY

*In this excerpt, critic Louis Breger claims that the memory
of an encounter with a physically abusive government official during Dostoyevsky's adolescence turned into raw material
for metaphorical expansion on the state of Raskolnikov's (and
by extension) Russia's state of mind.*

Raskolnikov, hero of Dostoevsky's novel *Crime and
Punishment*, conceives a plan to murder an old pawnbroker to
whom he is indebted. Just prior to committing the murder he
has a dream; he sees himself as an innocent young boy, watching with horror as a drunken peasant beats an old horse to
death. The dream contains an orgy of violence, along with
sympathy for the victimized mare and a sense of helplessness.
Raskolnikov awakens and immediately recognizes the connection between the dream and his plan: he has imagined smash-
ing the pawnbroker with an ax just in the way the peasant
smashes his horse; in both dream and plan the rage is directed
at a worn-out creature, a useless "old nag."

The dream of the suffering horse has become one of the best
known in all literature; its rich imagery expresses meaning on
many levels. Where, in Dostoevsky's own experience, might
some of these images come from? As he constructed his novels,
he recorded outlines, associations, ideas and drafts in notebooks; it is our good fortune that many of these have been preserved. In the *Notebooks for "Crime and Punishment,"* amidst
material dealing with the pawnbroker and the murder, we find
the line, "My first personal insult, the horse, the courier." This
is a direct link with the horse-beating dream and refers to an
event in Dostoevsky's adolescence that left a powerful and
long-lasting impression. He was fifteen and his mother had
died a few months earlier, after a protracted siege of tuberculosis. His father was taking him, along with his brother Mikhail,
from their Moscow home to the Academy of Military Engineering in Petersburg where, his father had determined, they would
train for practical careers. Military engineering was far from
the minds of the young brothers, aspiring writers who
dreamed of poetry, romantic dramas, and "Everything beauti-

purpose and then sent away. From the point of view of the infant Feodor, this woman who nursed him was his mother and weaning was accompanied by an actual loss. He then had his own mother, Maria, only to lose her to Varvara, the first of many sibling replacements. Aliona then joined the family and shared caretaking with Maria for the remainder

ful and lofty." Their romantic preoccupations were rudely interrupted when the carriage was stopped at an inn. They saw a government courier, a large man in an impressive uniform, drive up, rush into the station house for a glass of vodka, and return to a fresh carriage with a new driver, a young peasant. The courier then raised his fist and began beating the driver on the back of the head and he, in turn, lashed the lead horse with his whip. Dostoevsky describes his impressions some forty years later [in *Diary of a Writer*]:

> Here there was method and not mere irritation—something preconceived and tested by long years of experience—and the dreadful fist soared again and again and struck blows on the back of the head. . . . [The driver who] could hardly keep his balance, incessantly, every second, like a madman, lashed the horses. . . . This disgusting scene has remained in my memory all my life. Never was I able to forget it, or that courier, and many an infamous and cruel thing observed in the Russian people. . . . This little scene appeared to me, so to speak, as an emblem, as something which very graphically demonstrated the link between cause and effect. Here every blow dealt at the animal leaped out of the blow dealt at the man.

In the remainder of the article, Dostoevsky, moving to a metaphorical level says that "couriers no longer beat the people, but the people beat themselves, having retained the rods in their own court."

Dostoevsky was forty-four when he drew on this memory in writing *Crime and Punishment*; he was fifty-four when he recorded it in *The Diary of a Writer*. Whatever the actual events were at age fifteen, they had no doubt become blended with much that occurred earlier and later in his life. I am suggesting that we think of his account of the horse and courier not as a "memory"—as a literal rendition of fact—but as a story, a creation that weaves together emotions and themes from many different periods. It is like one of the "scenes" in Freud's case studies, like a particularly rich, compressed dream.

Excerpted from Louis Breger, *Dostoevsky: The Author as Psychoanalyst*. New York: New York University Press, 1989, pp. 1–2. (total pages: 295). Copyright 1989, New York University.

of his childhood years. I spell out these details to make clear that Dostoevsky experienced a series of losses early on in the sphere of maternal care. The pattern of multiple mothers also shows that his predisposition to splitting does not just stem from the good and bad aspects of one mother, but has a background in reality.

It would be convenient for the present interpretation if the real Aliona, like her namesake in *Crime and Punishment*, was a cruel and depriving woman. But, what evidence is available suggests a more complicated picture. She was very tall—like Lizaveta—with an immense appetite and an equally immense belly. She was not a serf but a Moscow townswoman who, like Katherine Marmeladov, found it necessary to stress her higher status in relation to the other servants and wet nurses.

Dostoevsky seems to have felt affection for this alternate mother, judging by comments he made in later years. Grossman reports that he "often recalled his own nanny, a Moscow girl, an 'unassuming woman,' amazingly noble in spirit, hired from among the petite bourgeoisie, who with dignity called herself 'citizenness'!"

Dostoevsky speaks of her in a letter to his mother, written when he was fourteen: "I am so sorry for Aliona Frolovna she suffers so much poor thing, soon she will waste away to nothing from the consumption she has caught."

Aliona was still living three years later so her consumption was probably just a cough, but Maria did, in fact, come down with tuberculosis at about this time. It was she who wasted away to nothing before the eyes of her grieving son, as his wife did many years later.

To sum up, there were various features associated with the real Aliona that led Dostoevsky to use her name for that figure in the novel who personifies the negative side of his maternal ambivalence. She was one of his two principal mothers and was tied to those aspects of his real mother that most aroused his helpless rage and guilt: tuberculosis and loss. In fact, the final loss of both these women occurred at the same time. Since she was a servant and the subject of his father's cruelty, she was a more acceptable target for aggression than Maria who—especially after her early death—was idealized by everyone. In addition, she seems to have been a living caricature of deprivation and oral greed, with her "wasting away" and huge stomach, words and sights that make strong impressions on young children.

While Aliona came to symbolize the hated mother in *Crime and Punishment,* the name Maria or Mary was a natural symbol for the idealized, loving mother. The Dostoevsky family were believing Christians and the young Feodor had a good deal of exposure to pictures of Christ and the Virgin Mary. The relationship between the biblical Mary and her perfectly loving son—as Dostoevsky imaged him—became an abiding ideal, a goal he strove for to the end of his life, as an analysis of the later novels will reveal. His daughter reports that he always kept a print of Raphael's *Madonna and Child* on his writing table.

As we have seen, *Crime and Punishment* presents an intense struggle with both sides of the maternal ambivalence. There is a major resolution in the novel, though versions of the conflict continue in other works. In *The Possessed,* Fedya—Dostoevsky's nickname as a child—murders Maria; who is a Lizaveta-figure, a loving, simple, woman.

THE HORSE AND COURIER MEMORY

It is intriguing to trace these associative links, but it can also lead to overinterpretation. Let us return to the horse and courier, an image connected with the rage and guilt that stand at the heart of *Crime and Punishment.* . . .

Dostoevsky places his memory of the horse and courier scene on the journey from Moscow that began just a few months after his mother's death. The departure for school marked the abrupt end of his childhood and the loss of the home in which he and his brothers and sisters grew up. Within two years his father would be dead—he never saw him again after he went to the academy—and the younger children dispersed among various relatives. Father was scheduled to take his two oldest sons to Petersburg, shortly after the mother's death, but the journey was delayed when Feodor developed a "mysterious illness . . . a throat or chest ailment whose diagnosis was uncertain." Dostoevsky's younger brother, Andrey, later wrote that, from the time of their mother's death and the strange illness, Feodor's voice always retained "a curious throaty quality which never appeared quite normal."

Dostoevsky himself does not mention his mother's death in relation to the horse-courier memory—nor anywhere else in his writing or correspondence as far as we know—

though he does make much of his mourning for Pushkin. It is my view that his idealized love for his mother was displaced onto Pushkin, whose death coincided with hers. This would explain why, of all writers, he idolized Pushkin to the end of his life. Pushkin was a great poet; he stands at the beginning of the masterful literature of nineteenth century Russia and many later authors felt a strong allegiance to him. Dostoevsky drew both inspiration and specific content from his work. (See, for example, the dream scene in Pushkin's *The Captain's Daughter* as a predecessor of the horse-beating dream.) Yet, while Dostoevsky was a discerning critic of most other authors—including those such as Gogol whom he admired—his praise of Pushkin seems one-sided, suggesting a leftover idealization. (See the speech he gave in 1880 at the unveiling of the Pushkin monument in *The Diary of a Writer.*)

Dostoevsky's mother's death had a profound impact on him and the emotions and images related to it were active when the horse-courier scene so impressed itself in his mind. What additional evidence suggests that this might be so? First, the death of a young mother is likely to have a strong impact on any fifteen-year-old. This was particularly so in this family where the father was the demanding authority and the mother the main source of affection. Her death marked the loss of the primary loving figure in his life. Yet, while outwardly idealizing her, there is much that indicates his powerful ambivalence: strong longings for her love, frustration over not obtaining enough, and a great deal of unconscious anger and guilt. All of these emotions would have been activated by her death; a prime indication is his throat and chest ailment, which sounds like an unconscious identification with his dying mother's tuberculosis. That is, it is an instance of how she was symbolically kept alive within him in an attempt to block the pain of loss and also punish him for his anger. Much is suggested by this somatic reaction to her death, including his capacity to experience external relationships vividly as if they were other selves, living within him.

The throat and chest symptom is not the only evidence that ties the horse-courier memory to the mixture of love, anger, and guilt stimulated by his mother's death. There is abundant material from the relationships with women later in his life, along with the way women are depicted in his fiction, in which these same emotions are played out. The analysis of *Crime and Punishment* has shown how Raskolnikov is driven by a powerful mixture of love and rage. The violence that breaks through so clearly in the horse-beating dream is the underside of Dostoevsky's feeling for his mother, the rage and frustration aroused by her illness and death. At the same time, the dream captures his horror at this feeling, his love for her, and his identification, the way he must also suffer her fate.

FATHERS AND SONS

While fathers have almost no place in *Crime and Punishment*, they do in Dostoevsky's other novels. His father played an important role in his actual development and a complete account of the horse-courier memory must include some comments on their relationship. At the time he witnessed the scene, he was being taken to the Academy of Military Engineering by his father, to be forced into a career that was completely foreign to his own interests, talents, and sympathies. The father, a former military physician, was by all accounts a most difficult man. Within his family he was moody and irritable, jealous and begrudging of his wife's time and affection, rigid and demanding with his sons. He never beat them physically, as far as we know, but did subject them to a great deal of verbal abuse and criticism. Like the mother in *Crime and Punishment*, the pawnbroker, Luzhin, and other hateful figures, Dostoevsky's father was a great inducer of guilt; he never tired of letting his children know how much he suffered on their behalf. From early in their lives, the Dostoevsky boys were subjected to strict academic demands; they had to learn Latin, geometry, memorize long passages, and perform for their father, and small mistakes brought forth his rage and insults. Of course, they were not allowed to react openly to this treatment; he was the authority and demanded obedience and respect. The placement in the academy was the culmination of their father's control of their education; he had decided, largely on the basis of his own insecurity about money and status, that military engineering was safe and profitable, and, with his characteristic lack of understanding of his sons' interests, was forcing this career upon them.

It is reasonable to assume that these emotional currents concerning his father were active on the trip to Petersburg and played their part in Dostoevsky's reaction to the horse and courier scene. He was being abused and insulted psychologically and could do nothing about it. He was filled with anger that he could not directly express at the authority who was running his life, as the courier ran his driver, and this reinforced his identification with the scene.

Dostoevsky's reaction to the scene illustrates several important aspects of his personal style. There is the capacity for powerful identifications, the way in which he experiences his own conflicts and feelings in and through the people and events around him. These identifications are multifaceted: he feels himself to be both horse and courier, victim and oppressor, as well as, and perhaps most, the driver, the one in the middle who is "insulted," knows what it means to suffer, yet cannot help passing the hurt down the line. We have seen this clearly in Raskolnikov's vacillation between sympathy for victimized women and the urge to attack them, and it is an abiding theme throughout Dostoevsky's fiction. An additional feature of his style is the way in which personal reactions are generalized into broad themes: social, national, even universal. He responds to the scene not only with his own feelings—which may have been too painful to think about directly—but also in terms of the Russian people. Both the capacity for identification and the universalization of the personal, in evidence at age fifteen, were to prove important when he later took up literature as the primary means of expressing his ideas and feelings.

Raskolnikov's Split Personality

Raymond J. Wilson III

Raymond J. Wilson III, professor of English at Loras College in Dubuque, Iowa, psychoanalyzes Raskolnikov and argues that he suffers from multiple personalities. Wilson cites an episode in which Raskolnikov mistakenly refers to one of the painters from Alyona Ivanovna's building by the name "Mikolka." This name appears earlier in the novel as a part of a dream that Raskolnikov had, and Wilson claims that this dream isolates the three personalities that exist and interact within Raskolnikov throughout the novel—a violent murderer, a disinterested onlooker, and a generous young child.

In trying to understand Raskolnikov's apparently erratic behavior in *Crime and Punishment,* readers have often resorted to the idea that Raskolnikov has a "split personality" even before they find out his name comes from the Russian root *raskol* meaning schism or split. However, the simple notion of a two-way Jekyll-Hyde or emotional-intellectual split in Raskolnikov never proved completely workable in analyzing Raskolnikov's personality. Raskolnikov cannot be forced into so limited a mold. The implications of Raskolnikov's horse-beating dream provide more flexibility for analysis. Aspects of the dream reflect facets of Raskolnikov's complex personality. This very flexibility, however, causes problems in interpreting the dream, as W.D. Snodgrass demonstrates in his analysis:

> First of all, where is Raskolnikov in his dream? Is he the horse, the little boy, the father, or the brute Mikolka? The answer must be Yes. All of the characters of the dream are the dreamer. The problem is not to decide who is who, but rather to understand the tenor of the dreamer's apprehension of the world, that is, of his mind. . . . For the horse, also, I have given

Excerpted from Raymond J. Wilson III, "Raskolnikov's Dream in *Crime and Punishment,*" *Literature and Psychology,* vol. 26, no. 4 (1976), pp. 159–66. Reprinted by permission of *Literature and Psychology.* (Notes and references in the original have been omitted in this reprint.)

what must seem disparate interpretations. Does the horse represent the teen-aged girls, Dunya and Sonia, Or does it represent the pawnbroker, the landlady and the mother, Or Marmeladov and Raskolnikov? Once again, the answer to all the questions is Yes. To miss the identity of all these characters as symbolized by the horse is to miss an essential texture of Raskolnikov's mind.

Obviously needed is a way to select, from this wealth of material, the aspects of the dream which best help us explain Raskolnikov's actual behavior, without over-simplifying the character by denying that other aspects exist. Confusion in the novel over the painter Mikolka's name helps us do this.

THE PAINTER WITH MANY NAMES

At the moment Raskolnikov is about to confess his murder to a police examiner named Porfiry Petrovich, a painter bursts into Porfiry's office claiming the crime as "mine alone." The painter's name creates confusion. In Dostoevsky's own words, not attributed to any character, the painter is "Nikolay," the name used by both the police examiner and the master worker who reported Raskolnikov's return to the scene of the crime. Raskolnikov's friend Razumikhin calls the painter "Mikolay" and "Nikolka." In the painter's confession scene with Porfiry, Raskolnikov alone calls the confessing painter "Mikolka." If we assume an error by the author, this confusion would be surprising. However, as Raskolnikov's mistake, the error provides a clue to our use of the dream material.

The name "Mikolka" links the painter to the Mikolka of Raskolnikov's horse-beating dream (Part I, Chapter 5). Raskolnikov dreams himself as a little boy feeling guilt and horror at his inability to prevent a drunken peasant named Mikolka from beating the animal to death. Like the painter, the dream Mikolka claims full responsibility for the crime, screaming, "You keep out of this! She's mine, isn't she? I can do what I like with my own." Raskolnikov had been about to reveal his murderer personality, prompted—like the dream's Mikolka—by anger and hatred. When the painter confesses, Raskolnikov listens instead to an inner voice urging him to act as if the crime were none of his business. This detached attitude is expressed in the dream by the little boy's father, an onlooker, who tells the little boy that the crime belongs to Mikolka and is none of the boy's business.

Each of the three main actors in Raskolnikov's dream—Mikolka, little boy, and onlooker—reflect ways of reacting that Raskolnikov consistently demonstrates in the novel. First the peasant Mikolka, who kills the horse, projects the Raskolnikov capable of a physically brutal axe-murder and of cruelly insulting those who love him. Second the little boy Raskolnikov, who cries agonized tears, represents the generous Raskolnikov aiding the Marmeladov family and the one who impulsively prevents a well-dressed man from pursuing a confused young girl. Finally there is the little boy's father in the dream who urges him to continue their walk to the graveyard saying, "It is none of our business. Let us go." The father has the voice of the uninvolved onlooker Raskolnikov who says, "What business is it of yours?" to the policeman he has just asked to aid the young girl. The same onlooker operates when Raskolnikov tells himself how "stupid" he is to give his money to the Marmeladov family.

THE THREE PERSONALITIES IN THE THREE INTERVIEWS

We see these three personalities in Raskolnikov's three interviews with the police inspector. In the first interview, Porfiry mainly deals with Raskolnikov's onlooker personality. Raskolnikov maintains a "none-of-my-business" attitude and deals successfully with a trick question about the painters, one of whom Raskolnikov later calls by the dream nickname. Raskolnikov evades this trick. But later we discover that his hostile tone of laughter at the beginning had enabled the magistrate to guess "everything then." Obviously Porfiry's trained ear detected the murderer's voice.

The murderer personality becomes even more important in the second interrogation, at the end of which Raskolnikov actually calls the painter by the dream nickname. On the way to Porfiry's office for this second examination, Raskolnikov "felt infinite, boundless hatred for him, and he even feared that his hatred would make him betray himself." Whenever Raskolnikov is in one aspect of his personality and has to shift suddenly to another, it shocks his emotional system. Porfiry intentionally evokes Raskolnikov's murderer personality, the result being that "At moments" Raskolnikov "longed to throw himself on Porfiry and strangle him then and there."

Porfiry's tactics make it difficult for Raskolnikov to keep from reacting like a murderer. At one point he "fell suddenly into a real frenzy . . . a perfect paroxysm of fury." Alternately, Porfiry shocks Raskolnikov by reminding him that the crime is supposedly none of Raskolnikov's business, by saying variations of: "Good Lord! What are you talking about? What is there for me to question you about?" Such reminders progressively upset Raskolnikov:

> As he had before, he suddenly dropped his voice to a whisper, instantly recognizing with anguish and hatred that he felt obliged to submit to the command, and driven to greater fury by the knowledge.

Finally Raskolnikov "rushed at Porfiry," who is quite delighted at this open display of murderous qualities telling Raskolnikov that he has already betrayed himself. But, before Porfiry can confront Raskolnikov with the implications of his actions, the painter bursts in to confess. The timing is pure coincidence. But Raskolnikov calls the painter "Mikolka" and this is not coincidence. For Dostoevsky employs the supposed error again.

In the third interview, Porfiry no longer tries to provoke the murderer in Raskolnikov. Instead, he speaks in a mild paternal tone evoking the little boy personality, urging Raskolnikov to drop his onlooker pretense. Notably, here for the first time, Porfiry calls the painter by the dream character's nickname: "No, Rodion Romanovich, my dear chap, Mikolka isn't in this at all!" Raskolnikov responds "like a frightened small child caught red-handed in some misdeed." He smiles "meek and sad" and speaks "as if he no longer could conceal anything at all from Porfiry."

In the sense we have been using, everyone has many parts to his personality. But in Raskolnikov's case important parts are alienated from each other. The onlooker cannot see how the old woman's death can possibly concern him. The murderer has sneering contempt for the little boy's acts of impulsive generosity. The little boy is totally horrified by the murderer's acts of brutality. This alienation gives meaning to the word "split" in the term "split personality." These are not postulated interior forces or images but overt ways of acting which the other characters recognize. The real test of the dream characters' explanatory value is whether they contribute to the reader's understanding of Dostoevsky's depiction of Raskolnikov. Eight important episodes demonstrate that they do.

RASKOLNIKOV'S REUNION WITH HIS SISTER

On seeing his sister for the first time in three years, Raskolnikov brusquely denounces her marriage plans. Those present make allowances for the insult because of his "condition," which we can see as the temporary dominance of the Mikolka personality. Dr. Zosimov later recalls this in terms that could apply to Mikolka: a "monomaniac, who had been goaded almost to raving madness by the smallest word. . . ."

But the next morning, Raskolnikov arises talking to himself the way the dream's onlooker talked of those who tortured the animal. In the dream the onlooker implies: What business is it of ours? He says, "They are drunk, they are playing the fool." And awake, Raskolnikov thinks:

> His most horrifying recollection was of how "ignobly and disgustingly" he had behaved, not only in being drunk, but in taking advantage of a young girl's situation to abuse her fiancé in front of her, out of stupid and hastily conceived jealousy, when he knew nothing either of their mutual relationship and obligations or, properly speaking, of the man himself. And what right had he to condemn him so hastily and rashly? Who had appointed him the judge?

The onlooker in the dream said: "It's none of our business. Let us go." Like him, Raskolnikov now says . . .

> of course, I can't gloss over or efface all this nastiness, now or ever . . . and so I must not even think of it, but appear before them in silence . . . and not ask forgiveness, but say nothing.

Yet, on seeing his mother and sister again, Raskolnikov makes all right again with the charm of a little boy—astounding the others present. Their mother's face "shone with pride and happiness" as she notes "how simply and delicately" Raskolnikov achieved the reconciliation. And his friend Razumikhin thinks: "Now that's what I absolutely love him for!"

THE MURDER ITSELF

Before the crime, the onlooker in Raskolnikov's personality tells him that he cannot possibly be serious in his plans—but not from any sense of moral outrage; rather, being split from the murderer, the onlooker feels no identity with the Raskolnikov who can be brutal. However, when the time comes, Raskolnikov, like Mikolka, strikes Alyona repeatedly with the blunt side of the axe. Raskolnikov then reacts in horror at his own crime just as the little boy of the dream reacts to Mikolka's cruelty. Lizaveta's arrival turns little-boy horror into terror; and as Raskolnikov flings himself forward with the axe "her lips writhed pitifully, like those of a young child when it is just beginning to be frightened. . . ." Lizaveta, like the old mare, responds minimally and ineffectively. And, as a voice in the dream had urged, Raskolnikov mercifully finishes her off with one blow from the sharp edge of the axe. Again Raskolnikov first reacts, like the little boy, with horror and repulsion for what he had done, rather than with "fear for himself."

In the dream the onlooker treats the crime as trivial: "'Come away,' said his father, '. . . Come away; don't look!'" And "It is none of our business. Let us go." After the crime, Raskolnikov turns more and more to this attitude:

> But a growing distraction, that almost amounted to absent-mindedness, had taken possession of him; at times he seemed to forget what he was doing, or rather to forget the important things and cling to trivialities.

Raskolnikov calmly washes his hands and cleans the axe, treating the bodies in the other room and the money in the bedroom as if they were none of his business. Near-discovery shakes him out of this mode. But as he escapes, we listen to an interior debate. One voice urges him to run, to hide in the doorway, to take a cab. The other, parallel to the dream's onlooker calms him and urges him to act as if nothing has happened.

RASKOLNIKOV'S MEETING WITH ZAMETOV

When he meets Zametov, the police clerk, at a bar called the "Crystal Palace," Raskolnikov tries to talk of the axe murder like an onlooker who can have only passing interest. But "in a flash he remembered, with an extraordinary intensity of feeling," the scene in the murder room. And he "was suddenly filled with a desire to shriek out, to exchange oaths with them, stick out his tongue at them, mock at them, and laugh, laugh, laugh." Raskolnikov's Mikolka personality makes Zametov shiver and recoil suddenly from Raskolnikov. Dostoevsky describes the result of the struggle between the Mikolka personality and onlooker in Raskolnikov's appearance:

> The latter's eyes were glittering, he had grown shockingly pale, and his upper lip trembled and twitched. He leaned as near as possible to Zametov and began moving his lips, but no sound came from them; they remained like this for half a minute. He knew what he was doing, but he could not restrain himself.

Zametov's obvious recognition of the murderer brings Raskolnikov "to his senses." The onlooker emerges again, and Raskolnikov successfully acts as if the murder is none of his business.

RASKOLNIKOV'S RETURN TO THE SCENE OF THE CRIME

When Raskolnikov leaves Zametov, the switches continue. Meeting Razumikhin at the door of the bar, Raskolnikov viciously insults him. Then he stands by, watching an attempted suicide as if it were none of his business, never even wondering if he should try to help. He goes to the murder scene where he must pretend that the crime is no business of his. Suddenly switching to the horrified little boy, he asks to be taken to the police. People hesitate and the commotion of Marmeladov's accident distracts him. He tries to help the man and impulsively gives all his money to the widow for the funeral. This little-boy generosity stirs Raskolnikov to great joy, but then his onlooker takes control and misinterprets, reinforcing the theme that Raskolnikov can go on living as if the crime were none of his business: ". . . it had come to him suddenly, as to a man clutching at a straw, that even for him it was 'possible to live, that life was still there, that his life had not died with that old woman.'"

THE CONFESSION TO SONYA

In the dream the onlooker had urged the little boy on toward the cemetery, a dubious course. And another insight by the onlooker demonstrates the limited life open to Raskolnikov if he continues clutching at the straw that the onlooker offered him at the Marmeladov's:

> "Where was it," Raskolnikov thought, as he walked on, "where was it that I read of how a condemned man, just before he died, said, or thought, that if he had to live on some high crag, on a ledge so small that there was no more than room for his two feet, with all about him the abyss, the ocean, eternal night, eternal solitude, eternal storm, and there he must remain, on a hand's-breadth of ground, all his life, a thousand years, through all eternity—it would be better to live so, than die within the hour? Only to live, to live! No matter how—only to live!"

In effect, the onlooker urges Raskolnikov to stay up on the cliff face, a disastrous choice. But Sonya urges him to try to climb down to the solid ground, as dangerous as that effort might be.

The little boy in Raskolnikov takes the first step down

when he confesses to Sonya. Raskolnikov must overcome the onlooker's urging him not to confess. But when Sonya begins to guess his secret, Raskolnikov "looked at her and suddenly in her face he seemed to see Lizaveta." The expression is that of a small child and Raskolnikov's little boy personality at last emerges. Dostoevsky supplies the italics to make this point more emphatic:

> Her fear suddenly communicated itself to him: the same terror showed in his face and he gazed at her with the same fixity and almost with the same *childish* smile.

Sonya's tender reaction brings tears to Raskolnikov's eyes and, "Long unfamiliar feelings poured like a flood into his heart and melted it in an instant." But on her vow to follow him to prison, Raskolnikov "felt a sudden shock" of the change of personality modes and "the old hostile, almost mocking smile played on his lips." In declining the offer, Raskolnikov no longer speaks as a little boy: "In his changed tone she now suddenly heard the voice of the murderer."

RASKOLNIKOV'S IMPULSE TO MURDER SVIDRIGAYLOV AND TO COMMIT SUICIDE

As more characters learn of Raskolnikov's murder—first Sonya, then Svidrigaylov, then Dunya—Raskolnikov finds the onlooker's indifferent position more difficult to maintain. The position erodes, leaving more and more the choice between murderer and little boy. At one point, the murderer seems dominant as Raskolnikov resolves "with cold despair" to murder Svidrigaylov. This proves unnecessary, but the murderer's most vulnerable victim may be Raskolnikov himself. The Mikolka part of him takes malicious pleasure in repeatedly striking a victim aspect of himself, just as the dream's peasant enjoys striking repeated blows. Raskolnikov even numbers his repeated psychological blows:

> '. . . Oh, aesthetically speaking, I am a louse, nothing more,' he added, suddenly beginning to laugh like a madman. 'Yes, I really am a louse,' he went on, clinging to the idea with malicious pleasure, burrowing into it, playing with it for his own amusement, 'if only because, first . . . secondly . . . thirdly. . . . Finally, I am a louse because, . . . Oh, platitudes! What baseness!'

The dream Mikolka killed the mare. There is a danger that Raskolnikov will kill himself. As Svidrigaylov puts it, "Rodion Romanovich has two ways open to him: a bullet through the brain, or Siberia." Raskolnikov contemplates suicide on the canal at the very moment that Svidrigaylov actually kills *himself.*

Raskolnikov's Last Interview with His Mother

Turning sharply away from suicide at the canal, Raskolnikov proceeds immediately to his mother where his "heart was all at once softened" just as at his confession to Sonya. Then Sonya had knelt at Raskolnikov's feet; now with his mother, Raskolnikov "fell down before her and kissed her feet, and they wept, with their arms about one another." Her reaction makes clear that the little boy possesses his personality then:

> 'Rodya, my dear, my first-born,' she said, sobbing 'now you are just like the little boy you used to be; you would come to me just like this, and put your arms round me and kiss me.'

Raskolnikov repeats this gesture a year later falling at Sonya's feet and accepting "resurrection into a new life" at the feet of the woman whom the other prisoners called, "Little mother." Like a little boy he is free to start a new life. That evening Raskolnikov for the first time combines the objectivity of the onlooker with the warm emotion of the child:

> Everything, even his crime, even his sentence and his exile, seemed to him now, in the *first rush of emotion*, to be something external and strange, as if it had not happened to him at all (my emphasis).

The onlooker has never before been described as having strong emotions. This is a more whole, more complete feeling and indicates a process of reintegrating the split-off parts.

Raskolnikov's Final Confession to the Police, and the Eventual Reintegration of his Personality

The three parts of Raskolnikov's dream also explain Raskolnikov's confusing final confession scene, resolving it into the interplay of specific personality fragments. Raskolnikov has decided that he cannot act as if the crime were none of his business. First, too many people know about his guilt; and second, he cannot live like a man on a ledge of a cliff—he must confess to start a new life. But he has not repented. Saying goodby to his sister Dunya early in the very day of his confession, Raskolnikov repudiates her suggestion that he is "half atoning for your crime" by "advancing to meet your punishment." Raskolnikov's contempt for his victim still resembles the dream Mikolka's contempt for the old mare.

> 'Crime? What crime?' he cried, in a sudden access of rage.
> 'Killing a foul, noxious louse, that old money lender . . . was
> that a crime? That is not what I am thinking of, and I do not
> think of atoning for it.'

Raskolnikov feels sorry only for the stupidity of his failure.
Thus even as he prepares to confess, Raskolnikov claims he
still feels as if he had committed no crime. His sister's response
indicates her frustration at his inability to grasp the implications of his own action. "'Brother, brother, why are you saying
this? You really did spill blood!' cried Dunya, in despair."

Raskolnikov then visits Sonya to bid farewell. He goes to
her, as he realizes moments later, out of Mikolka-like cruelty. "I wanted to see her terror, and watch her heart being
torn and tormented!" But as Raskolnikov leaves Sonya's
apartment, a desperate renewal of the onlooker wonders, "Is
it really impossible to stop now and revise all my intentions
again . . . and not go?"

Suddenly remembering Sonya's advice to "say aloud to all
the world, 'I am a murderer!'" Raskolnikov has a shuddering
change "like a clap of thunder" and "tears gushed out." To admit the murder as his crime, while not in the murderer aspect
of his personality, would be a step towards unifying the split-
off parts. Raskolnikov "almost flung himself on the possibility
of this new, complete, integral sensation." Desire for completeness, for this integral sensation, brings the split parts
close enough to allow Raskolnikov to fall on his knees in the
Haymarket. But comments by bystanders, that he is a drunk
or a pilgrim to Jerusalem, encourage the onlooker by acting
"as a check on Raskolnikov" stilling "the words 'I am a murderer,' which had perhaps been on the tip of his tongue."

Raskolnikov's need for a "complete, integral sensation," to
be obtained by claiming the murder, suggests the importance
of confession for Raskolnikov. It is not the act of confessing
that is important but the consequences. By confessing
Raskolnikov would publicly and irrevocably claim the murderer as part of himself. In addition to any good feelings the
confession might give him, claiming the murderer would
make it part of his public identity. His position as prisoner
would give him the sustained public identity of "the axe murderer," making the shift to onlooker difficult. For a whole
year after confessing, Raskolnikov will resent this identity.
But the prison situation relentlessly forces Raskolnikov to ac-

cept the reality that he did murder the old lady, this being prison's main therapeutic quality. Only when Raskolnikov finally accepts this reality can the little boy's triumph pave the way for the slow emergence of coherent personality.

But there is danger that Raskolnikov will not confess. For personality switches continue even after the Haymarket insight. When Raskolnikov enters the office of Ilya Petrovich, this police clerk chatters on treating Raskolnikov with such complete implicit assumption of innocence that the onlooker powerfully revives in Raskolnikov. The police officer does not even exactly remember Raskolnikov's name, creating a temptation to try again to act as if the murder were "none of his business." Svidrigaylov posed the greatest threat to reveal Raskolnikov's secret. News of his death removes another obstacle to the onlooker's position, further tempting Raskolnikov to turn back. Raskolnikov staggers out of the office, but the sight of Sonya renews the little boy personality that had sent Raskolnikov into the office. He returns and confesses.

CHAPTER 4

Dostoyevsky's Treatment of Philosophical Issues

The "Unstable" Nature of *Crime and Punishment*

W.J. Leatherbarrow

W.J. Leatherbarrow, professor of Russian and Slavonic studies at the University of Sheffield in England, defends Dostoyevsky against the charges of critics who have argued that his characters are unrealistic and unlikable. Leatherbarrow claims that Dostoyevsky made a number of modifications in his drafting process that were departures from the literary conventions of the day. Among the most important of these are the adoption of a "selectively omniscient narrator" and the unstable nature of the narrative, which Leatherbarrow argues warps the way in which the reader perceives time, space, and other characters in the book. Leatherbarrow identifies Svidrigaylov and Sonya as the only two characters—other than Raskolnikov—whose depiction escapes this instability, a status that makes them particularly suitable representatives of the "paths" that Raskolnikov can choose to follow in changing his life at the end of the book.

The first reference we have to the work that was to become *Crime and Punishment* is to be found in a letter Dostoevsky wrote to his brother in October 1859, where he refers to a novel in the form of a confession upon which he is about to embark and which will make his name as a writer. His return to St Petersburg and subsequent participation in the journalistic world clearly distracted him from this early intention, for it is not until 1865 that he again mentions a project identifiable with *Crime and Punishment.* In June of that year, in a state of considerable financial embarrassment following the deaths of his first wife and brother and the failure

Excerpted from Introduction, by W.J. Leatherbarrow, to *Crime and Punishment,* by Fyodor Dostoevsky, translated by Richard Peavar and Larissa Volokhonsky (New York: Everyman's Library, 1993). Reprinted by permission of the publisher.

of *The Epoch*, his second journalistic venture, Dostoevsky wrote to A.A. Kraevsky, the editor of *Notes of the Fatherland*, asking for an advance of three thousand roubles against the manuscript of a novel to be entitled *The Drunkards*. This novel was to deal with family deprivation and the current problem of drunkenness in Russia, and although Dostoevsky's plan offered no hint of the central character, plot or theme of *Crime and Punishment*, it clearly outlined material he was later to work into the Marmeladov sub-plot when Kraevsky eventually refused this offer. In September 1865 Dostoevsky wrote from Wiesbaden to M.N. Katkov, editor of the journal *Russian Herald*, describing a project clearly recognizable as the first draft of *Crime and Punishment*. . . .

This letter clearly sets out details of the main plot and central characters of what was to become *Crime and Punishment*: it presents the student Raskolnikov and his victim, the pawnbroker Alyona Ivanovna; it offers tantalizing glimpses of the character conceptions which were to be fleshed out with such artistry into the lascivious landowner Svidrigailov, the pawnbroker's meek sister Lizaveta, and Raskolnikov's own mother and sister. The references to the action taking place 'in the present year' and to the student's delusion by 'half-baked ideas that are in the air' suggest that Raskolnikov's crime was conceived on the basis of the rational utilitarianism advocated by Chernyshevsky and the other men of the sixties. Dostoevsky's clearly stated intention that his hero should discover 'unsuspected and unanticipated feelings', which 'destroy his convictions' that a murder may be justified on the basis of the greater good of the greater number, mark this novel out as an attempt to oppose the morality of the nihilists with Christian morality itself.

Dostoevsky worked upon *Crime and Punishment* for the remainder of 1865 and throughout the following year, starting it in Wiesbaden and completing it in St Petersburg. It was published in installments in *Russian Herald* between January and December 1866. Much of the work on the novel was carried out in the most adverse personal circumstances. As well as the deaths of his wife and brother in 1864, Dostoevsky had to contend with the financial implications of the collapse of *The Epoch* and his own pathological addiction to gambling. Matters were further worsened by a recurrence of his epilepsy and the threat of debtor's prison. His dire financial position had forced him into an unfavourable contract with the unscrupulous publisher Stellovsky, which obliged him to break off work on *Crime and Punishment* for three weeks in September 1866 in order to dash off a shorter novel, *The Gambler.* Moreover, in November 1865, dissatisfied with what he had written so far, Dostoevsky had torn up his manuscript for *Crime and Punishment* and started afresh. Readers who wonder at the breathless, agitated, and intense nature of his novel need only consider the conditions under which it was composed.

All of the foregoing makes it clear that *Crime and Punishment* was rooted in the historical and intellectual climate of its time, as well as in personal experience and the circumstances of Dostoevsky's own life. It is important to consider these factors, but it is equally important to recognize that they alone do not account for the greatness of this novel. *Crime and Punishment* continues to stimulate successive generations of readers not because it revives the ideological disputes of the 1860s or reflects the personal and philosophical tribulations of the author's life, but because its consummate artistry invests it with universal meaning and allows it to transcend the particularities of its conception. The novel grew under Dostoevsky's pen, and the themes and characters outlined in the Katkov letter gradually acquired a complex life of their own. The mysteries of the artistic process dissolved the author's straightforward polemical intentions in an altogether more imaginative and stimulating concoction.

Raskolnikov's "Uncertain" and "Unstable" Character

In particular, Dostoevsky's conception of the motive for Raskolnikov's crime changed dramatically during his work on the novel, becoming progressively more challenging. The final result represents an intriguing inversion of the conventions of the detective novel: in *Crime and Punishment* we know from the start the identity of the murderer, so that the reader's interest is focused instead on a quest for his elusive aims and motivation. The Katkov letter makes it clear that Raskolnikov's crime was originally conceived as an enactment of the utilitarian morality of the nihilists: in what he regards as a rational and justifiable adjustment to the social order, the hero kills and steals from a rich and useless hag in order to benefit a larger number of needy and potentially more useful members of that society. Yet, in the novel itself, Raskolnikov quickly discovers that not only does such utilitarianism fail to justify his crime in the face of those unanticipated sensations of disgust and guilt which surface after its commission, but, more startlingly, it does not even account for his behaviour during the crime itself. If he really murdered in order to make more advantageous use of his victim's wealth, why then did he not discover in advance the precise value and location of her belongings? Why does he abandon his gains after the crime? Why is he tempted to betray himself to those who knock at the pawnbroker's door after the murder? Above all, perhaps, why does he never seriously contemplate the possibility of robbery without murder? Such questions haunt the murderer in the days after his crime, revealing the irrational depths of his own behaviour, promoting agonizing self-analysis and gradually disclosing to him that his 'theoretically justified' crime was in reality an inexplicable act of murderous violence, not a neat piece of social surgery.

As the novel unfolds other potential motives for the crime emerge from the enigma of Raskolnikov's personality, undermining further his original belief that a criminal act may be consciously carried out on the basis of a single, rationally conceived theory. From his article on crime, which he discusses with the investigator Porfiry Petrovich, we learn of Raskolnikov's belief that humanity may be broadly divided into two classes: the *supermen*, such as Napoleon or Newton, who, because of their innate moral, intellectual or historical superiority, may claim the natural right to overstep conventional morality and law in order to accomplish their historic mission; and the *lice*, who are the building blocks, not the architects of progress, who contribute little, if anything, to human development, and who therefore are bound by legal and moral conventions. Such a theory must inevitably tempt Raskolnikov into a harrowing dilemma of self-definition: to which group does he belong? Is he a man or a louse? Does he have the right to overstep, or does his ordinariness condemn him to obedience? This dilemma lies at the heart of his personality and his crime. A man of immense pride and solitude, he values his moral freedom; but, at the same time, he is constantly visited by doubt and is mindful of his need for other people. When we encounter him at the start of the novel his soul is tormented by this uncertainty to such a degree that we come to suspect that the murder of the pawnbroker is conceived as the key to resolving this crisis of identity. It becomes, perhaps unconsciously, a test through which Raskolnikov attempts to achieve self-knowledge and to define his own status, an act of overwhelmingly personal, rather than social significance. As such a test it fails, and Raskolnikov remains uncertain both of who he is and of why he has murdered. Only in the novel's Epilogue, when he has embarked upon penal servitude and the long path to redemption, is he granted revelation. Yet his spiritual rebirth and religious conversion, as outlined in these final pages of the novel, inevitably provoke scepticism. After several hundred pages of Raskolnikov as a lost and despairing murderer, the final resolution seems too neat and psychologically unconvincing. It represents, for most readers, the overt intrusion of the author's views, a 'pious lie' (Mochulsky) on Dostoevsky's part, and a desperate effort to nudge his hero into God's camp.

The uncertainty with which Dostoevsky invests his portrayal of Raskolnikov's personality and motivation is extended to include other aspects of the novel. Indeed, when Robert Louis Stevenson read *Crime and Punishment* in 1886, he remarked that the reader's impression of delirious confusion was rather like enduring an illness. Raskolnikov's taut and anguished consciousness fills the novel to such a degree that we lose sight of any objective sense of what is really going on. This was a deliberate artistic aim on Dostoevsky's part and it helped to determine his eventual choice of narrative structure. The manuscript he abandoned towards the end of November 1865, covering the events of Part One, had been written in the form of a first-person confession. This, of course, was entirely in accordance with his original intention, as outlined to his brother in October 1859. The problem with first-person confessional narrative, however, was that although it allowed direct access to the inner workings of the hero's mind, it afforded real technical problems when it came to filling in details of the external world. It required the hero to witness an event, or at least to hear an account of it himself, before he could describe it. Such restrictions compelled Dostoevsky to try something new—a selectively omniscient narrator, able occasionally to witness events Raskolnikov cannot, but who is for the most part compelled to share the subjective uncertainty of the hero himself. The choice of this technique allowed Dostoevsky to blur the very nature of perception in *Crime and Punishment.* The function of the narrator as merely another confused participant in the fictional world inevitably raises questions about the way he presents such fundamental features of that world as time, space, events and characters. Put more simply, we cannot trust what we appear to encounter in this novel. Our proximity to Raskolnikov's subjective and indistinct vision means that if he is confused, then we are confused; if he does not know what is dream and what is reality, then we cannot know. We are rarely afforded the opportunity to measure his experience against more objective criteria; we are thus compelled to participate in an intensely subjective world, which is arguably closer to our own experience of life than the measured narrative objectivity of other realist novelists.

This unstable quality of *Crime and Punishment* may be illustrated in a variety of ways. Time, in particular, is warped by Raskolnikov's experience of it. Locked in the hero's mind we lose all sense of objective duration, and it comes as a surprise to be reminded that the whole action of the novel, excluding the Epilogue, lasts only two weeks. It seems much longer than this for the simple reason that time is painfully drawn out for Raskolnikov himself. Our sense of space is similarly distorted: Raskolnikov's room, tomb-like and oppressively minute as he lies in bed, haunted by ideas, sickness and guilt, turns out to be surprisingly spacious as it accommodates a seemingly unending procession of visitors. The city of St Petersburg itself, with its oppressive dirt and heat, its narrow alleys and dingy taverns, seems like an externalization of the hero's claustrophobia and an extension of his pathological state of mind. Indeed, throughout the novel we often cannot tell where Raskolnikov ends and the outside world begins. The topographic details of the city are absorbed in the hero's consciousness and transformed into a psychic landscape haunted by the ghosts of his imagination.

OTHER CHARACTERS IN THE NOVEL

These 'ghosts' include many of the novel's secondary characters. One of the most distinctive features of *Crime and Punishment* is the elusive and unstable nature of the personalities with whom the hero comes into contact. Rather than a gallery of robustly independent secondary characters, such as we encounter in the novels of Tolstoy, we are confronted by what appear to be emanations of Raskolnikov's own thought processes. His conviction that mankind may be divided into the strong and the weak, the Napoleons and the lice, those who may transcend law and morality and those who may not, discolours his, and therefore our, perception of the people around him. When, for example, in Part One, Chapter 4, Raskolnikov sees in the street a young girl about to be violated by an older man who is clearly indifferent to the moral connotations of his behaviour, he regards them in the light of his theory and his response is correspondingly ambiguous. His initial distaste for the immoral 'transgressor' and sympathy for the weak victim of his will is soon inverted, as he urges the policeman to let events run their course. In a similar fashion the two victims of Raskolnikov's crime—the grasping and self-centred Alyona and the meek and abused Lizaveta—also echo both Raskolnikov's theory and his own dualism. To a lesser degree his mother and sister fit this same pattern: Dunya is strong-willed, while the mother is weak and compliant.

However, the two most compelling external reflections of Raskolnikov's divided nature are the monstrous landowner Svidrigailov and the meek prostitute Sonya. Each of these characters quickly loses the quality of 'otherness', in the sense of a separate and objective identity, and they become symbols of the choices confronting the hero. Svidrigailov embodies the qualities of the Napoleon, albeit in a form that Raskolnikov finds loathsome. He possesses the same moral freedom and indifference to the conventions of law and morality that mark out the superman. He regards others as disposable means for the realization of his designs, and it becomes clear that he has played some part in the deaths of his wife and servant. Raskolnikov is inevitably drawn to him, and the fact that his distaste for Svidrigailov grows in the course of the novel is just one example of the 'unsuspected and unanticipated feelings' Dostoevsky planned for his hero in the aftermath of the crime.

Raskolnikov is just as strongly drawn to Sonya. Her humility, self-sacrifice and unwillingness to challenge the divine order, even though that order appears to have condemned her to a life of suffering and self-loathing, is in stark contrast to Svidrigailov's demonic assumption of moral autonomy. The moment when Raskolnikov confesses his crime to Sonya, unaware of the fact that Svidrigailov is also listening in, is a dramatic confirmation of the interdependence and symbolic importance of the two characters. The moment is a crucial one in the novel, designed to highlight the paths open to the hero. Dostoevsky's notebooks show that he at one point intended Raskolnikov to follow Svidrigailov down the path of moral independence, despair and eventually suicide. The relevant entry reads: 'The end of the novel. Raskolnikov goes off to shoot himself.' Dostoevsky's discarding of this option in favour of the suffering and redemption advocated by Sonya allowed not only the conventional happy ending intimated in the Epilogue, but also the opportunity to invest the novel with a positive moral charge.

The fact that the peripheral characters in *Crime and Punishment* are so strongly coloured by the hero's expectations and frame of mind also raises interesting questions about the examining magistrate Porfiry Petrovich, who pursues Raskolnikov so skillfully and finally confronts him with his guilt. Porfiry is immensely proud of his professional skills and psychological insight, and our first reaction is perhaps to admire him for his doggedness and uncanny perspicacity. There is, however, another way of approaching him. Dostoevsky made it clear in his letter to Katkov that his hero was to feel a moral need for punishment; and indeed, after the crime Raskolnikov does appear to go out of his way to provoke suspicion against himself. He revisits the scene of the crime and arouses the suspicions of the housepainters; he faints at the police station when the murder is being discussed; and he deliberately toys with the police clerk Zamyotov when he meets him in a tavern, coming very close to an overt confession. The way Raskolnikov is so attracted by the lure of capture and punishment should alert us to the possibility that Porfiry Petrovich's omniscience might exist only in the hero's tormented mind, and that this character, like so many of the others, is a dislocated fragment of the criminal's consciousness, stripped of his own identity and obliged to play out the whims of his manipulator. The careful reader will readily identify several occasions when Porfiry's speech and thought patterns reflect uncannily those of Raskolnikov himself, and all will question the detective's strange 'disappearance' from the novel after he has finally elicited from his quarry an admission of guilt.

THE REACTION OF DOSTOEVSKY'S PEERS

In the final analysis, *Crime and Punishment* is an exciting tale, compellingly told. It enjoyed considerable critical and popular acclaim when it was serialised throughout 1866, alongside the early installments of Tolstoy's *War and Peace.* Yet its hallucinatory, frenzied and melodramatic quality, as well as its treatment of the darker sides of both Russian reality and human psychology, must inevitably have raised questions about the nature of Dostoevsky's genius, particularly in the light of Tolstoy's measured, epic depiction of Russian life in both its historical and domestic contexts. Despite its apparently melodramatic excesses, there is much in *Crime and Punishment* that marks it out as a work of realism: as well as its depiction of contemporary intellectual life, it offers a convincing portrait of the lower depths of nineteenth-century St Petersburg existence. The current problems of drunkenness, urban poverty, inadequate housing, prostitution, social inequality, and legislative reform are all woven indelibly into the novel's fabric. Dostoevsky himself was more than pleased with the work's social accuracy, being especially encouraged by contemporary newspaper reports of crimes committed in circumstances similar to those described in the novel. But Dostoevsky's credentials as a realist were often challenged by others. As early as the 1840s [Russian critic Vissarion] Belinsky had criticized Dostoevsky's capacity for dramatic excess and grotesque fantasy. This charge stuck, to be repeated by many subsequent readers; even Tolstoy (who, oddly enough, never met his great contemporary) remarked on the implausibility and exaggeration of Dostoevsky's art, as well as on his taste for perverse, unhealthy and wholly unrepresentative characters. Similar criticisms were made by his earliest foreign readers: [Irish poet and playwright] George Moore dismissed *Crime and Punishment* as a melodramatic penny-dreadful 'with psychological sauce'; the *Spectator*, reviewing *The Idiot*, expressed revulsion at 'this so-called realism which consists in a display of deformities, more or less hideous, dragged forth and paraded for the public to gloat over'; [early–twentieth-century British novelist] D.H. Lawrence concluded that Dostoevsky was 'not nice' and was 'like the rat, slithering along in hate, in the shadows, and in order to belong to the light, professing love, all love'; while Lawrence's contemporary John Middleton Murry, who wrote one of the earliest English studies of Dostoevsky, argued that his works were not true novels and did not represent life, but were instead outpourings of 'metaphysical obscenity'.

Such views are far removed from Dostoevsky's own accounts of his artistic aims and achievements. He certainly recognized that, unlike many other realistic novelists, he avoided in his works strict verisimilitude and a preoccupation with everyday trivialities, preferring instead to concentrate upon abnormal characters in extreme situations. But he defended this choice, conceding that 'I have entirely different notions of reality and realism from those of our realists and critics', and arguing that 'what most people regard as fantastic and exceptional is sometimes for me the very essence of reality'. In a comment in his notebooks, written towards the end of his life, he went even further, declaring: 'I am a realist in a higher sense; that is, I depict all the depths of the human soul.' As we read *Crime and Punishment* more than a century after it was written, we are compelled to recognize the accuracy of Dostoevsky's 'higher realism' and to admire his penetrating insights into the life not only of his time, but of ours as well. There is nothing remotely faded or 'bookish' about this novel; in its perceptive treatment of crime, violence, urban neurosis, split personality, spiritual uncertainty, and moral and social disorder, it speaks as loudly to our own age as it did to Dostoevsky's. The figure of Raskolnikov, the murderer/intellectual prepared to sacrifice fellow human beings on the altars of theoretical premises and his own satanic pretensions to moral freedom, is startlingly modern and by now distressingly familiar. Today's reader may no longer find it so easy to accept the confident solution to Raskolnikov's moral disorder offered in Dostoevsky's Epilogue, but he cannot fail to admire the unprecedented psychological insight with which this disorder is exposed before our gaze.

Fate as Divine Will in *Crime and Punishment*

David Matual

David Matual, professor of Russian at Wright State University in Dayton, Ohio, argues that fate determines Raskolnikov's motive for murdering Alyona Ivanovna. Matual argues that, in his notebooks, Dostoyevsky viewed the murder as something of a "necessary evil" for Raskolnikov's ultimate spiritual regeneration.

To prove his theory, Matual discusses the number of "coincidences" that happen to Raskolnikov and how these may represent the workings of some force beyond human control, whether that force is named "fate" or "God."

In several passages of *Crime and Punishment* and especially during the confession scene with Sonia in Part V, Chapter 4, Raskolnikov attempts to clarify the motive which has impelled him to murder and rob the old pawnbroker, Alena Ivanovna. His difficulty in identifying the cause of his actions makes him one of the most fascinating and bewildering characters in world literature—a criminal in search of a motive, as Philip Rahv once observed. The first suggestions of a motive are made at the very beginning of the novel in the numerous references to the hero's penurious condition. The nineteenth-century Russian critic Dmitrii Pisarev accepts these allusions at face value and asserts that Raskolnikov kills for money alone. Pisarev's explanation is undermined by the hero's failure even to count the money he has stolen. Nevertheless, the financial factor must not be rejected out of hand. Raskolnikov's impoverishment is, if not the direct motive of his crime, the background against which his malevolent idea is conceived. A second motive, adumbrated in Part I and elaborated in Part V, is the so-called humanitarian mo-

Excerpted from David Matual, "Fate in *Crime and Punishment*," *International Fiction Review*, vol. 3, no. 2 (July 1976), pp. 120–25. Copyright ©1976 by the International Fiction Association. Reprinted with permission. (Endnotes in the original have been omitted in this reprint.)

tive. Alena Ivanovna is a scavenger living on the helplessness of her clients. The profits reaped from her usurious
rates will go to a monastery after her death. Early in the
novel Raskolnikov overhears a student tell a young officer
that the murder of such a woman is an insignificant price to
pay for the confiscation of her wealth and its distribution to
the needy. Arithmetic justifies such a course: one life is lost
(and a useless one at that) while thousands are saved.
Raskolnikov is struck by the proposition because he himself
has been thinking the very same thing. A third explanation
of the crime—the "great man" theory—is found in the hero's
article on crime and the psychology of the criminal. According to its central thesis certain men are ordained by history
to accomplish momentous tasks, and, in order to reach their
goals, they are empowered to bypass conventional morality
and violate any rule that obstructs their way. Raskolnikov
explains his Hegelian notion to Sonia in Part V, but discovers
that he cannot accept it any more than she can understand
it. The reader, however, must not dismiss this argument too
quickly, for Dostoevsky himself attached considerable importance to it. In a long letter to his publisher he outlined the
plot of *Crime and Punishment* and characterized his hero as
a young man beguiled by certain "incomplete ideas" es-
poused by the members of his social milieu. This motive,
like all the others, has a firm foundation in the data of the
novel. For Raskolnikov truly believes, or wishes to believe,
that he is such an extraordinary man, living beyond good
and evil. A fourth explanation of the crime is akin to the
"great man" theory. It views the hero's actions as an assertion of free will and the autonomy of the individual—themes
which occupy a prominent place in several of Dostoevsky's
earlier writings, especially in *Notes from Underground.*
Raskolnikov says that he committed the murder for himself
alone, that he wished to prove that he was not a louse but a
man, i.e., a *free* man. In view of the author's preoccupation
with the theme of volitional freedom it is not unreasonable
to give this motive its due consideration. A fifth motive is
also worthy of comment. Raskolnikov commits murder, it is
claimed, because he is seeking suffering for himself. His numerous verbal and biographical ties to such spiritual
masochists as Marmeladov, Katerina Ivanovna, and especially Mikolka, the young peasant who confesses to the
hero's crimes, make this explanation quite plausible. Ac-

cording to a sixth explanation Raskolnikov's unbalanced
state of mind leads him to the perpetration of the crime. Because the narrator alludes so frequently to his hero's delirious condition before and after the murder, this theory also
contains an element of truth. Indeed, the greatness of *Crime
and Punishment* is at least partially attributable to the multi-
plicity and validity of all the motives either adduced by
Raskolnikov himself or suggested by the novel's events.

AN ALTERNATE EXPLANATION: FATE

There is still another explanation of the murder to be considered. It too seems valid to me, although it has often been
denigrated and rejected by critics and scholars. Raskolnikov's crime may be seen as the result of the direct and indirect intervention of an external, supernatural force. At various places in the novel it is called "fate," "God," or the
"devil," but they all amount to the same mysterious power.
Evidence for this motive is abundant especially in Part One,
which presents the history of the crime, and in Part Six,
when Raskolnikov begins the long journey toward his spiritual conversion.

The account of the crime and the events that lead up to it
is a veritable history of good fortune and fantastic coincidences, all of which the hero attributes to a force beyond
himself. When he visits the pawnbroker for a "test," he
eludes the attention of several janitors. In a subsequent
episode he walks to the outskirts of the city, falls to the
ground exhausted, and has a dream in which an old horse is
flogged to death by a band of drunken peasants. Upon awak-
ing he cries, "Thank God, it's only a dream." These words
are quickly followed by the incredulous plaint: "God! Can it
really be, can it really be that I will actually take an axe, hit
her on the head, and shatter her skull? That I will slip in her
sticky, warm blood, jimmy the lock, steal, and tremble and
hide all covered with blood? With an axe? Lord, can it really
be?" After the dream he picks himself up and heads back for
his apartment. He is now free, the narrator tells us, from
"this spell, the sorcery, the charm, the obsession." Yet unac-
countably he does not go home directly but passes instead
through Haymarket Square, where he learns by chance that
Lizaveta, the pawnbroker's half sister, will be gone that
evening and Alena Ivanovna will be in the apartment alone.
Hearing this, he feels "like a condemned man" and "sud-

denly with all his being he felt that neither his reason nor his will were free any more and that everything had been settled for good." Later, when Raskolnikov looks back on his circuitous journey from the outskirts of Saint Petersburg to his room and the conversation casually overheard on the square, he explains the entire incident as the "predestination of fate." From the very beginning of his murderous idea he sees the "presence of certain special influences and coincidences." It is by chance that he first learns of Alena Ivanovna; it is by chance that he hears a conversation between an officer and a student passionately declaring the utter futility and harmfulness of her existence; and it is by chance that he has been entertaining the same thought.

Raskolnikov is struck, even horrified by the information he gleans from the conversation in Haymarket Square. Even more striking is the manner in which it is conveyed. A tradesman and his wife tell Lizaveta to come to their place "in the seventh hour" (*v semom chasu*). The same standard Russian word for "seventh"—*semoi* instead of *sed'moi*—occurs later just before Raskolnikov leaves his room for Alena Ivanovna's apartment. While he is fussing with the false pledge he will use to avert her suspicion, an unidentified voice from the courtyard alerts him: "It's long past six!" (Literally, "It's been the seventh hour for a long time," *Semoi chas davno*). In the original, the coincidence is perfectly obvious, although Raskolnikov does not notice it. Nor does he notice that the abrupt and urgent cry goading him to action suggests even more persuasively than the other chance happenings of Part One that a mysterious external power is deeply involved in his thoughts and deeds. The narrator makes this even clearer as the moment of the murder approaches. Raskolnikov feels "as if someone had taken him by the hand and pulled him, irresistibly, blindly, with supernatural force, without objection. It was just as if the wheel of a machine had caught a clump of his clothing and begun to pull him in." After leaving his room, he finds an axe under a bench. He does not merely see it; it *shines* to him as if to call attention to itself. No one notices him take the object. His explanation of this stroke of luck points once again to his persistent faith in preternatural powers: "If reason fails, there's always the devil." Fortune seems to smile on him again when he passes through the gate to Alena Ivanovna's building, for a haycart entering before him conceals him from the gaze of the people on the street. After killing the pawnbroker and her half sister, Raskolnikov takes temporary refuge in a vacant apartment on the second floor. Some painters had been working there earlier, but now they have left "as if on purpose." The hero returns to his own building, replaces the axe without being seen, and retires to his room. Everything appears to have come off without a hitch. His every step has been guided and even constrained, or so he believes. Dostoevsky, through the thoughts of the hero, the words of the narrator, and the events antecedent to the crime, has created, it would seem, a very cogent case for the theory of an external force as a prime mover in the plot of *Crime and Punishment.*

Nevertheless, this theory has had little success with those who have written on Raskolnikov's motivation. In a recently published collection of critical essays on *Crime and Punishment* Robert Louis Jackson argues that in order to explain the myriad of happenstances and coincidences the hero has recourse to the notion of fate because he has lost all faith in God or in the meaningfulness of God's world. The "fate" Raskolnikov has come to believe in is nothing more than the inevitable consequences of his own behavior, "the iron logic of his own, inner fatality." The Soviet critic G.M. Fridlender takes a similar position. In his view the theory of fate is a reflection of the hero's emotional state and is therefore a corollary of the highly dubious theory of madness. Konstantin Mochul'skii, who has written the most perceptive study of Dostoevsky's *Leben und Werk* ["Life and Works"], compares Raskolnikov with the tragic hero of antiquity perishing in a vain struggle with Fate. He can be saved, it is argued, only through faith in Christ; without that faith he becomes the plaything of destiny.

The most troublesome and ultimately most unsatisfying element in these remarks is the assumption that God and fate are *opposed* to each other. It is, of course, quite true that Raskolnikov has abandoned God and that he frequently imputes his crime to the power of fate. But by the same token can it be maintained that God has abandoned *him* and ceased to be a part of his life? It seems quite possible to me that Raskolnikov has incorrectly identified the external power that besets him and that what he regards as a sinister force is in fact the benevolent action of God's grace. The question of the role of fate in the novel should be treated not solely in terms of its psychological validity; rather, it must be viewed in the context of the problem of good and evil and of Dostoevsky's notion of theodicy [trying to justify belief in God despite the experience of evil].

Raskolnikov is, as [German historian and literary critic] Walter Schubart has claimed, a "sinner full of grace," who passes "from crime through repentance to rebirth." Why "crime"? Dostoevsky is surely not suggesting that crime—in this case murder—is the *sine qua non* of spiritual regeneration, but for Raskolnikov it becomes the first step on the difficult road to salvation. In his study of Dostoevsky's Christian *Weltanschauung* Nikolai Losskii contends that evil and its objectification in crime are never absolute. Either they contain an element of good or they create those circumstances which favor the triumph of good. To be sure, all depends on the attitude of the criminal. If moral good is alien to his nature, if he fails to feel the slightest remorse after his crime, the process of regeneration is frustrated and nullified. This is hardly the case with Raskolnikov, however. *Crime and Punishment* is replete with references to his piety as a child and his acts of kindness as an adult. (Consider, for example, his aid to the young girl about to be raped by the stranger, his solicitude for the Marmeladov family, and his defense of Sonia at the funeral repast.) These periodic manifestations of good combined with his frequent feelings of revulsion toward the crime both before and after its commission make him susceptible, as it were, to the effect of divine grace. But the ultimate goal of palingenesis cannot be achieved without the ordeal of suffering, or in the words of Nikolai Berdiaev, "only great suffering occasioned by evil can raise a man to a greater height." Raskolnikov can ascend that height only by assuming suffering, and he suffers only because he feels more and more keenly the discrepancy between his criminal behavior and the innocence of an earlier existence which is fortified by Sonia's love. She and the positive characters in the novel mirror the conflict in his heart and prefigure the ultimate victory of good.

LAZARUS AND THE THEME OF REGENERATION

It is not without reason that the Biblical story of the raising of Lazarus plays such a central role in the book. The theme of physical resurrection presented in the tale is ultimately bound up with Raskolnikov's conversion, for he is portrayed as a latter-day Lazarus. Before his first interview with the police inspector Porfiry Petrovich he decides that he will have to "sing Lazarus." The Russian phrase *pet' Lazaria* means "to complain of one's troubles." Raskolnikov means only this and nothing more. Yet his phraseology underlines this most vital theme of *Crime and Punishment.* During the ensuing conversation Porfiry Petrovich asks him whether he believes in the Biblical miracles, especially the supreme miracle—the raising of Lazarus from the dead. Raskolnikov answers affirmatively. The subject of their discussion obviously remains on his mind, for in a later conversation with Sonia he wishes to read the same story from her New Testament. Unable to find it, he lets Sonia read to him. Her measured and appropriately emphatic tones clearly indicate that she is aware of the parallel between the gospel account and the drama unfolding before her. When she reaches the verse in which Martha, the sister of Lazarus, tells Christ that her brother has been lying in the tomb for four days, she vigorously stresses the word "four." The same number is associated with Raskolnikov and his doubles in numerous contexts. The Russian word for "tomb" (*grob*) is equally significant in this passage. On an earlier occasion Raskolnikov's room is compared to a coffin. The importance of this detail is evident only in the original because Russian uses the same word for "tomb" and "coffin." Like Lazarus, Raskolnikov is in his tomb waiting to be summoned forth. In the light of these parallels the hero's spiritual resurrection in the epilogue appears not only justified but inevitable.

Regeneration is the teleology of *Crime and Punishment.* The importance Dostoevsky attached to it can also be seen in his notebooks. In an early version reference is made to the fact that Raskolnikov's mother used to read the gospel to him and that for some reason the words "Talitha koum" ("Get up, little girl") are lodged in his memory. The passage he remembers so faintly is found in Mark V: 41. Jairus, an official of the synagogue, implores Jesus to heal his daughter. When he reaches her bedside, however, she has already died. Assuring the family that the girl is only asleep, he commands her to rise and she obeys. The miracle of resurrection is a lingering memory in the notebooks; the story of Lazarus is the spiritual *dynamis* [Greek word meaning "with strength," used by a priest in Orthodox religious service to exhort a congregation to increased spirituality] of the finished novel.

What then does God have to do with the perpetration of the crime and the regenerative process it initiates? There is much evidence to indicate that God *wills* the murder, however unconventional and even blasphemous that position may seem. It is not that evil for its own sake is part of the divine plan; it is the consequences of an evil act that matter. The fundamental Christian myth of resurrection, so prominently represented in *Crime and Punishment* by the story of Lazarus, is centered in the belief that without evil and death there can be no resurrection; without suffering there can be no joy. The evil represented in the novel by the murder of Alena Ivanovna and Lizaveta is the instrument of Raskolnikov's salvation. In the notebooks we find this curious statement, which does not, however, appear in the final text: "Inscrutable are the ways in which God finds man." In this case the "inscrutable way" is crime. In more positive terms the notion of spiritual resurrection is found in this note, which appears under the heading "The Main Idea of the Novel": "He went to the Marmeladov girl [i.e., Sonia] not at all out of love but as if he were meeting with Providence." In the final version this note is attenuated somewhat, but the theme of providential guidance is still there. Raskolnikov goes to Sonia to confess his crime, and the narrator observes: "Pensively he stopped before the door asking himself a strange question: 'Do I have to tell her who killed Lizaveta?' The question was strange because at the same time he suddenly felt that not only could he not help telling her but that it was impossible even to postpone this moment even temporarily. He still didn't know why it was impossible; he only *felt* it, and this agonizing awareness of his impotence in the face of necessity almost crushed him."

Of all the critics who had addressed themselves to the question of God's role or the role of "fate" in *Crime and Punishment*, Jean Drouilly has given, perhaps, the most insightful explanation. "If Reason," he says, "cannot prevent the murder of a contemptible, useless old money-lender, God is there to give the gesture its true meaning. These seem to be the theses maintained by Dostoevsky in his *Crime and Punishment*."

Despite the persuasive evidence in the notebooks and the plethora of suggestive detail in Part One there is still no solid foundation for a theory of fate or divine intervention. The notebooks are not, after all, the novel itself but a series of false starts, experiments, and ideas. As far as the striking coincidences and chance occurrences in Part One are concerned, they can all be dismissed, as Jackson and Fridlender maintain, as the hero's attempt to rationalize his own predetermined course of action. Far more convincing arguments in favor of the theory of an external force are presented in Part VI, when Porfiry Petrovich confronts Raskolnikov for the last time. The police inspector represents at first the law of man in pursuit of a criminal and gradually emerges as a spokesman for the law of God as well. He not only perceives God's role in the whole affair but understands the necessity of the suffering which Raskolnikov must endure. Convinced that God has brought Raskolnikov to this denouement, he remarks: "So, I've been waiting and watching, and God is giving you over to me: you are coming to me." After formally accusing Raskolnikov of the murder, he speculates that God may have been "waiting for this" [i.e., the murder] and later adds: "Perhaps you still have something to thank God for. For all you know he might even be saving you for something." Porfiry Petrovich quite clearly believes that God not only does intervene in the affairs of man but that he will guide Raskolnikov's steps to confession, effect a conversion through the loving influence of Sonia, and lead him to the "new story" suggested in the final paragraph of the epilogue.

The Contradictions of Raskolnikov

David Hanan

Raskolnikov's psychological torment in *Crime and Punishment* stems largely from the fact that his philosophy of life is inherently contradictory. Raskolnikov then projects these contradictions on the world he sees around him, thereby making everything subject to his own necessarily flawed beliefs. David Hanan, a senior lecturer in film and television at Australia's Monash University, argues that Raskolnikov mixes several opposing concepts—such as hate and love, equality and superiority—making his problems the embodiment of the philosophical and sociopolitical turmoil that existed in nineteenth-century Russia. Hanan argues that Raskolnikov's belief system is made up of bits and pieces of so many competing moral and ethical theories that its violent expression (in the murder of Alyona Ivanovna) is almost inevitable, triggered by as simple an act as overhearing a conversation.

Dostoyevsky is not obviously an economical writer. In *The Possessed* he tends to circumscribe his meaning, balancing and weighing one social attitude against another. In *Crime and Punishment* the process is one of continual qualification—so that one statement can come to include something like its opposite, personal eccentricities are rapidly embraced by the anomalies of the whole social world, and yet the writing still leaves room for the unexpected:

> He was so badly dressed that any other man in his place, even if he were accustomed to it, would have been ashamed to go out in the daytime into the street in such rags. It was true, though, that in that particular part of the town it would be hard to astonish anyone by the kind of clothes one wore. The proximity of the Hay Market, the great number of disorderly

Excerpted from David Hanan, "*Crime and Punishment:* The Idea of the Crime," *Critical Review*, no. 12 (1969), pp. 15–28. Reprinted with permission.

houses, and, most of all the working-class population which crammed these streets and alley-ways in the centre of Petersburg, lent so bizarre an aspect to the whole place that it would indeed be strange to be surprised at meeting any man, however curiously dressed. But so much bitter contempt had accumulated in the young man's heart that, notwithstanding his occasional youthful fastidiousness in dress, he was least of all ashamed of his rags in the street. He would, no doubt, have felt differently if he had met some of his acquaintances or former friends, whom, as a rule, he was not very fond of meeting. And yet when a drunken man who for some unknown reason was being taken somewhere in a huge empty cart drawn by an enormous dray-horse, suddenly shouted at him as he drove past, "Hey, you there, German hatter!" and began bawling at the top of his voice and pointing at him, the young man at once stopped in his tracks and clutched nervously at his hat.

Even here, where it appears possible to be absorbed into the anonymity of such a dense and [diverse] world, one can still find oneself very much a marked man. It is to this effect, too, that Dostoyevsky plays on our sense of constriction and over-crowding, so conducive to the wantonness of city life, in the image of the drunken man who is still subject to fits of ill-temper and bawls at the top of his voice at Raskolnikov.

The whole treatment of Raskolnikov proceeds on similar principles. He is a contradictory figure, and the narrative *can* only proceed, not by an attempt at accounting definitively for motivation, but rather by action and dialogue, by registering the movements of thought—that is, by presenting all the features of his behaviour, shaped so that a pattern will ultimately emerge. It is for the reader to make sense of that pattern, to lay bare that underlying psychic continuum wherein the action is finally intelligible. The difficulty is that some of the key contradictions can only be rendered in passages which, although immensely suggestive, are as mysterious as the psychic states they describe. Here, for instance, is Raskolnikov's reaction on reading his mother's letter describing her own and Dunya's misfortunes:

Almost all the time he was reading the letter, from the very beginning, Raskolnikov's face was wet with tears; but when he had finished it, his face was pale and contorted, and a bitter, spiteful, evil smile played on his lips. He put his head on his old pillow and thought a long, long time. His heart was beating fast and his thoughts were in a whirl. At last he felt stifled and cramped in the yellow cubby-hole of his, which was more like a cupboard or a box than a room. His eyes and his thoughts craved for more space. He grabbed his hat and went out, without worrying this time whether he met anyone on the stairs or not; he forgot all about it. He walked in the direction of Vassilevsky Island along Voznessensky Avenue, as though he were in a hurry to get there on some business, but, as usual, he walked without noticing where he was going, muttering and even talking aloud to himself, to the astonishment of the passers-by, many of whom thought he was drunk.

What strikes one here is the curious and unexpected movement from sympathy—a sympathy which in Raskolnikov is perhaps very close to morbid involvement—to spite; not only spite, though, but a bitter, spiteful, evil smile, suggestive of resentment, calculation and delight. Where has it come from, what does it contemplate, against whom or what is it directed? If one feels him mastered here by emotions over which he has no power, one is still forced to wonder to what degree the state at which he finally arrives is self-induced ("He put his head on his old pillow and thought a long, long time. . . . At last he felt stifled and cramped . . ."). Or is it rather that he waits upon that moment when he *will* be overcome? And yet, even given that, does one still want to say that he is truly aware of what is happening to him? For there is something very puzzling indeed about this condition wherein feelings of pity, sympathy, compassion, involvement in the situations of others, can be swiftly and inexplicably transformed into their opposites: indifference, detachment, aggression, and conscious cruelty. The questions one wants to ask about Raskolnikov here are typical of those one wants to ask about his behaviour in the novel as a whole.

A young man, oppressed by his own circumstances and by those of others, living in a city permeated by the unsubstantiality of its human beings, takes an axe and, though he can't really tell where his own obsessions end and other people begin, murders an old woman who has become for him the symbol of injustice, meaninglessness and superfluousness—a superfluousness and meaninglessness that threaten his own life and the lives of those around him; yet a woman who also, in the end, remains anonymous, whose life he does not really know, though he thinks he can account for it. A brutal, irrational, perhaps ultimately inexplicable act of violence, it is also the desperate gesture of one with nowhere to turn: a man who has felt himself becoming the agent of a higher justice, and is prepared to bear responsibility for the sufferings of all men. For Raskolnikov will not only take into his hands the power of life and death, he will take into his own soul the suffering incurred in the murder of the old woman. He is a man with a sense that things are utterly wrong, and a genuine desire that they should be otherwise—although this oddly enough with him takes the form of hatred. Perhaps the old woman was vicious; she was also some sort of human being, a living and suffering anonymity.

And having committed his crime against the city, having murdered her, he finds that for him the whole city with its anonymous and insubstantial shapes rises up angrily, accusingly, and yet sorrowfully.

Towards the end of the novel, the detective Porfiri Petrovich says, and in doing so recapitulates something of the tone of the work: "We're dealing with quite a fantastic affair here, a sombre affair, a modern one, a case characteristic of our times. . . ." *Crime and Punishment* may not be Dostoyevsky's greatest novel, but in it, together with *Notes from Underground*, we see the beginning of his questioning of the religious and political dilemmas of our time—an exploration that was only to end with *The Brothers Karamazov* and Dostoyevsky's death some fifteen years later. For my part, I suspect that, despite his extended analysis of the state of alienation into which Raskolnikov is thrust by committing the murder (there is a sense in which he is more cut off before the murder than after it), and for all the resolutions that Dostoyevsky seeks to apply, the crime—or rather, the tensions it acts out and the questions raised by them—is more interesting than the punishment. For if, as we have seen, the crime is felt to have been done out of a desire for justice, the act itself is nihilistic and undermines the very possibility of the righteousness it seeks. What are we to make of that contradiction, and how does it relate to the society in which it occurs? There is surely no question whether Dostoyevsky condones such an act; we are forced, all the same, to ask why it is he is so imaginatively compelled by it.

ST. PETERSBURG AS A PROJECTION OF RASKOLNIKOV'S MIND

I want to begin by asking why it is that the phrase "instability of human beings", first quoted by Philip Rahv in his article "Dostoyevsky in *Crime and Punishment*," so compellingly evokes one's sense of the novel's world. For it seems to me that the novel has a quite uncannily phantasmagorical way of perceiving the world and, consequently, other people.

It is not fantasy we have here: uncertainties are real threats, and phantoms move from paranoid anonymity to real propositions. Typically, other people emerge into consciousness from out of states of delirium on the part of the perceiver; they appear menacingly, like figures in dream, mysterious, shadowy, yet strangely marked and calling attention to themselves. They themselves emerge from anonymity and can as quickly disappear back into it; they therefore feel to the reader, even when immediately before him, potentially anonymous, as everyone in the city is. And while they are always threatened with the anonymity of the street from which they materialize, they can be discovered to share—like Svidrigailov and Raskolnikov—a common destiny, to relate to each other in some secret way. The city like a human psyche is at once an inexhaustible source of related experience, yet continually exhausts its inhabitants, multiplying experience, emptying and threatening it with anonymity.

We see, then, that the novel not only puts the world of St Petersburg before us, but gives us a particular sense of that world. One of its most distinctive features is the way in which Raskolnikov, the central consciousness in the book, habitually projects his own preoccupations on to the world around him; and this indeed is not surprising, given such a shadowy unrealized population—they exist passively, their latent shapes wait upon, provide the objects for, projection. Yet the inescapable fact is that very often they answer to the truth of that projection. So that while they can, at significant points, discount it, often one has the sense of other people being seen most *really* at the moment when Raskolnikov projects his own psychic preoccupations onto them. Repeatedly the drama of an incident is focused most sharply when other people occur as figures within Raskolnikov's own mental life: the dramatic movement includes a shock of recognition, as a figure appears to declare itself once and for all, definitively, for what it is. Such incidents as the confrontation with the gentleman roué pursuing the drunken waif through the streets, Marmeladov's story of Sonia's plight, Raskolnikov's mother's letter, the dream of the old mare beaten to death—all of which repeat interminably the endless cycle of oppressor and oppressed—can only maintain Raskolnikov's conflicts and develop his impulse because they confirm *his* sense of the world—indeed, proclaim it for the reader. We are thus drawn into a world (both psychic and external) in which enormities continually declare themselves. And while we may feel that Raskolnikov is obsessed, such incidents, once perceived, exist as a threat not simply to him but to all: for not only have they *not* been resolved in his psyche, neither have they been resolved or accounted for in the world; and the novel itself projects this double fact with the reinforcing power of obsession.

So that while it is true to say that the city only exists through Raskolnikov's consciousness, and it is his sense of the city that we largely have, I would also argue that he is the city's consciousness, or rather its most definitive consciousness, as indeed he is its conscience, though this last term is by now ambiguous.

One of the features of the St Petersburg world that confirms Raskolnikov's impulse, and thus becomes a factor on his path to the murder, is the theory he so strangely overhears, even as he is forming a similar plan in his own mind; the theory outlined, significantly enough in the context of Russian history, by a student to a soldier: that such a person as the old woman money-lender may be killed and her money used by the young, the energetic, and the unselfish to build a new and better world; that, according to utilitarian principles, the humanitarian end justifies the means, and the greatest happiness is provided for the greatest number. Yet the odd thing about the theory in its statement here is that, in this case at least, though no one seems to realize it, the destruction of a human being is not a necessity: stealing would do as well, since all that is demanded is that certain resources be made available for social progress. It is indeed one of those sinister cases where the proponents don't seem to realize the nature of their own preoccupations. For while they talk of humanitarian ends, their real interest is in constructing a situation wherein they have the right and the motive to do away with another human being.

HOW TO BE SUBSTANTIAL IN A WORLD OF SHADOWS

It is significant that a theory invoking a crime against "superfluous people" should occur in this population of shadows. And once such a theory has arisen and is very much "in the air", such a society will soon find its Raskolnikov. He is drawn to its actualization, and it is here that we come to the second, major unrecognized implication of such a theory. "Well, in my opinion if you're not ready to do it yourself, then it's not a question of justice at all," is the soldier's reply; and while that is the view of common sense, what must be said about such a proposal is that it is only when it is acted upon by someone, that anyone at all comes face to face with its real consequences, consequences that otherwise are simply not imagined: namely, that the power of life and death is put into one man's hands. A person faced with the fact that someone is to be annihilated decides that he himself has the right and power to do it, and the decision as to who is to be annihilated rests in his hands. He must decide. And who, as Dostoyevsky asks in *The Brothers Karamazov*, can have that power?

Raskolnikov, of course, thinks he can. If people are indeed anonymous until proved otherwise, then one way of testing that life is a reality is to see it become a death:

> She uttered a cry, though a very faint one, and suddenly dropped to the floor, though still managing to raise her hands to her head. In one hand she still held the "pledge". It was then that he struck her again with all his strength, and then again, every time with the back of the hatchet and across the crown of the head. Blood gushed out as from an overturned tumbler, and she fell straight on her back. He drew away to let her fall. . . .

Here if anywhere Raskolnikov is driven to find his own tangibility in an act which, in proving the tangibility of others, binds him to a world of consequences and causality far greater than simply the moral. Yet the very shockingness with which this deed is performed before our eyes tends to hide its causes from us, replacing *them* with its own ultimate nature and the completeness with which it is done and seen. The rest of the novel is there, and is needed, to display those causes and the effect with which they permeate the murderer's society.

I think that in a very simple way Raskolnikov does believe in the social efficacy of his theory; it is a theory his own society offers to him; and the manner in which Dostoyevsky chooses to present it—outlined just before the murder, objectively narrated as part of a whole incident from the past and not as something immediately before Raskolnikov's mind—compels us to take it seriously: not as a convenient rationalization, but as something that its auditor thinks might well be tried out. Yet by the time we come to it, it is not this theory which is foremost before *our* minds, but the drive of a man possessed with the idea of murder. The first Book of the novel, right from the start, is pervaded with the momentum of strong and dark obsession in the process of realizing itself. So that when we do come to the theory it is related, for all its reasonableness of exposition, to a compulsion to exercise that power over life and death that has grown up as the deed itself approaches realization; the theory now is drawn back into a momentum of which it was but one initiator, while the compulsion itself is imbued with a sign, the stamp of the society that has put the idea before Raskolnikov. Despite the consuming subjectivity of the obsession, it is not he alone who is capable of imagining it.

It is at this point that we may see in what way the novel is about "an affair characteristic of our times". It is as though a whole psycho-social condition is worked out through Raskolnikov—as though through him is expressed Dostoyevsky's sense of a Daimon [or "Demon"] that has infected the city. That city nurses within itself the germ of an idea whereby any one of its members may take upon himself the right to annihilate another (potentially, any other) member, on its—society's—behalf. What we have here, though, is more than an idea: it is what I want to call a Daimon because it is an idea that has been imagined only because it has already, in some sense, been desired; once imagined, because of the nature of what has been imagined, because needed to be imagined, it is thereby already itself a motive power, impelled to manifest itself in events, and coming to rest only when the city that has produced it realizes what it has created in its midst. Just as Raskolnikov's sense of the world finds issue in the crime, so too the city culminates the *novel's* sense of the world, and in such a way that the crime is a culmination of the city.

RASKOLNIKOV'S MOTIVATION FOR MURDER

As might be expected, much of the critical discussion of *Crime and Punishment* has fixed on the question of motivation. The problem has been highlighted by Philip Rahv, when in his article he says of Raskolnikov: "he is in a state of fatal self-contradiction, in that he attempts to further a common end of an altruistic character with egotistical and purely private means." Yet while everyone is struck by this opposition between self-willed contempt for others on the one hand, and on the other Raskolnikov's preoccupation with bringing about good, most critics proceed to simplify the novel, either by explaining away one side of his character, or by preferring to see that character as contradictory, ultimately inexplicable, in accordance with its "modernity". Edward Wasiolek in his Introduction to *The Notebooks for Crime and Punishment*, claims that the "'pretty' humanitarian motive" is only an apparent motive: It is "flattering to Raskolnikov, evasively presented to the conscious mind as a rationalization of an ugly truth". Again, Joseph Frank concludes that "the whole point of the book lies precisely in the process by which Raskolnikov moves from one explanation of his crime to another" and so "discovers the truth that he committed the crime for himself alone, and solely to see whether he was strong enough to have the right to kill". . . .

Certainly, one comes away from the novel with a strong sense that egoism is an important dimension of Raskolnikov's character. Yet that sense is largely given us after the murder. Until then, he really is a man possessed; later, the personality is forced to take upon itself a wide variety of roles, attempting to account to itself for what it has already done. And if that in the end is a further form of egoism, it is a very strange form indeed. By then, though Raskolnikov is intensely preoccupied by moral possibilities, moral life in him has been so twisted into the circuit of the self that all possibilities assume distorted and terrifying shapes. He cannot work out a relation to himself without discovering his self in relation to what it has done to others.

Even in its form before the murder, however, egoism is not the only motive to propel him forward, for most of the situations by which Dostoyevsky depicts the path to the murder are pre-eminently moral in kind: the plight of the Marmeladov family, the exhortations and subtle demands from his mother, the incident of the girl in the streets—in every case he is drawn into what confronts him. Radically disturbed by these suffering lives, he realizes that on a social scale their plight is the plight of thousands; and even as this enjoins on him a heightened sense of responsibility, the situations themselves strike a chord of quite morbid sympathy, impossible to resist, but arousing other, more sinister psychic impulses. Characteristically, in fact, his cruelty is most marked on occasions where his sympathy and responsibility are called for or have already been activated. Thus we find that sudden and pointed indifference to the drunken waif being shadowed through the streets by the roué—a situation that seemed initially to horrify and outrage him:

The whole thing was as plain as could be. The gentleman was a smartly dressed, corpulent, thick set man of about thirty, the picture of health, with red lips and a small moustache. Raskolnikov became furious; he suddenly felt like insulting the fat dandy. He left the girl for a moment and went up to the gentleman.

"Hey you! Svidrigailov! What do you want here?" he shouted, clenching his fists and laughing, his lips foaming with rage.

He seems able neither to watch nor act without hatred and self-hatred. He expresses his moral outrage in the form of an insult; and the result of that is that it is he himself who takes the burden of the insult. He insults his own sense of moral outrage. Raskolnikov is a moral creature in so far as he is unable to bear his own intense moral perceptions.

THE JUSTIFICATION FOR THE MURDER

Of course, by the time the novel opens he is already possessed by his crime, and that is why he is unable to admit his moral feelings here: he can't bear them because he has already refused to bear them. He is involved in murder. However that is no explanation—for if these early strange transformations in his character occur as a consequence of that decision, they only re-exemplify, with immediacy, the mysteriousness of his initial nihilism. Why murder? Why has he, a man disturbed by the suffering he sees around him, turned to murder as a way out of that dilemma?

No complete answer seems possible. The novel, I feel, ultimately finds this pattern of behaviour mysterious, even as it sets it up as the main problem for analysis. The murder-instinct rises from within a confusion of spontaneous urges and theoretical considerations—a response to a particular case, but a case perceived with such intensity of feeling that a rush of new impulses is suddenly released. And that is typical of Raskolnikov's society, as well as of the man himself. So, even [in Part I, Chapter 6] as the student describes the treatment to which Alyona Ivanova subjects her sister, Lisaveta, and outlines the theory to which that case seemed to give rise, he gives way to a viciousness that, in its emotional quality and accent, goes well beyond any reasoned presentation of a theory. His tone remains unaccounted for, even though the theory as it emerges will seem to cover just such a case as this. . . .

A number of factors that lead Raskolnikov to the crime are

displayed by the student. Some of them I have already mentioned; and as the passage continues there is a growing sense of the unreality of the old woman's life: she herself is felt not to know what she lives for. Yet the effects of her life are clear enough; and that sudden loathing unto death that surges up immediately on contemplating her power over the unresisting Lisaveta is at once a desire for justice, and—as though he has suddenly taken *her* violence into himself, and more—a desire to strike her down with a violence commensurate to her own, until she, the aggressor, has been thrust into the same relation to him as Lisaveta was in relation to her. *Put her down, and make off with all she so graspingly possesses.* A moment later, as the conversation proceeds, justice will seem within the easy reach of optimism; yet now justice and revenge are too closely intermingled. . . .

We can see how the theory can accommodate such viciousness. For us, the readers, there is a quite shocking leap for the mind from humanitarian ideals to the brute fact of murder. For them, the proponents of such an idea, there is a necessary connection set up between the two: whenever they think of their society changing they always conceive of murder. And that is the most plain and inexplicable fact the novel puts before us.

Still, in some small but crucial way, perhaps the victims of this "social progress" help make their own deaths inevitable. The very way in which the old woman holds and guards her world invites attack. So bound up in her property and power, so defined by them, is her life, that dispossession will become for her a kind of death in any case. She will resist—would rather die, maybe, than give over what has become her nature, her world, her life; and perhaps what Raskolnikov intuits is that he must destroy that nature—greed—in order that her instinct for amassing may not start all over again. In killing her, however, he is acting to *overthrow* the principles on which his society stands, not merely to improve them; it is just this that he cannot see. He wants to commit the perfect crime—justifiable in conception, rational in execution, and one in which his own emotions are not involved; a crime the morality of which has already been decided by the theory, yet whose nature remains untested until the crime itself has been undertaken; a crime that *he* manages to undertake only because he does not really believe himself capable of doing it. Yet even as its prospect becomes imminent, so does his psyche cast up that dream of the old horse being beaten to death, wherein all those instincts hitherto suppressed rise up and make the reader, at least, aware that it is impossible for Raskolnikov to prevent himself feeling the suffering that he occasions. There is a sense, therefore, in which the man knows this, so that when he comes to the murder he is not simply denying the relevance of morality and human feeling, but actually trying to kill them.

The matter is however more complex than this. There are two things involved here: a morality which declares that one must not kill; and the corollary of this, that even the most meaningless, destructive and seemingly redundant life has a right to its own existence. Raskolnikov has loathed the old woman not only because she is unjust but also because she is the living embodiment of the injustice and meaninglessness that seem to threaten his own life as well as the lives of those around him. He is thus not only attempting to kill in his own mind a morality that he knows does exist for him— Thou shalt not kill—he is also trying to do away with a morality that allows such a *sense* of injustice and wasted lives to continue unchanged. He wishes not just to suppress or kill it in his own mind, but actively to see if it can be dispensed with. So the murder, though self-evasive, is also exploratory. Raskolnikov refuses to accept a state of affairs where good people suffer and die and, short of inhumanities perpetrated on the rest, there is nothing one can do about it. In so far as he refuses to accept that state of affairs or support any principle that upholds it, the murder is an act on behalf of love. The trouble is that he is not just violating a sense or a principle, he is killing a human being.

How the Contradictions Come Together

Yet while the motive of that murderous protest may be defined as partly one of love (even as it is also self-love), equally it must be said that it issues as an act of spite: spite against the old woman for necessitating and inviting murder, spite against himself because he can conceive of life in no other terms, spite against the whole order of things where murder seems the only possible method of social change, spite particularly because there still lives within him a morality that forbids what he has already undertaken to do. So twisted and turned back upon themselves are the impulses, that the murder appears even as an act of rebellion and spite against itself: *may I destroy myself and the old woman, my whole world, in this murder, because they and I leave me no other alternative but to conceive of it, and kill.*

That conception of murder issues not as a blow struck with hatred and self-hatred in the name of love, but as something even more intricate and perverse than that: a desire to put an end to the whole unbearable complex—hatred and self-hatred, love and self-love—out of which the present action, and perhaps others in the future, might have come. With the first blow the crime rejects that impossible tension which has given it birth, and becomes a protest against his whole dilemma. During the murder, Raskolnikov's experience is both one of pure will—the assertion of self against his world—and, in a universe for the moment morally dead, the yielding of self to something already determined upon. The act is utterly mechanical. With the ensuing rush of strength, his whole being is given over to the physical state, going with it so that the body becomes its act, like falling from a cliff. Yet even in this ultimate gesture towards freedom, the experience *will* become a sense of loss as much as concentration and discovery—and the act ends in space and unrelatedness. Even an act of self-will, it seems, must have its partner, without whom the deed resolves itself into a simpler kind of egoism: "he drew away to let her fall"—self regarding the power it once had over another. The supramoral state reverts to the criminal state it has, in a way, never left behind. For in what sense can one say one "loves" humanity when one loves it to the point where one can't accept its failings, and must annihilate not only the image of those failings, but human beings themselves?

As though in answer to that question, the novel shows how a man who is not by inclination a murderer, and of whose tendencies one can give no pathological account, becomes a murderer by the very terms his world gives him if he is to live in it. And once murder is the central fact of his world, then the *idea* of murder unleashes its own possibilities, and the man, not essentially a criminal, thereby becomes one and steeps himself in the murderer's pathology. As the only conceivable solution, murder generates its own hatreds, and in doing so makes life finally impossible for any moral being. Because he *is* a moral creature, he must now feel hatred for his whole sense of the world, including the murder in which it culminates. Thus men are corrupted by the tragic facts of their situation, even as they strive to create a bearable society—until the great political demand, "How can I make a better world for myself and others?" becomes co-extensive with the solipsism, "How can I make the world bearable for myself?" The endless cycle of oppressor and oppressed, always intolerable, is now ended in the unconsciousness of an act of pure being; but the man who at this point reaches for such release involves himself in the condition once and for all: in that blinding moment he does feel his own ultimacy and his escape from his oppressive vision, but the cycle is now completed, made actual in the world in its ultimate form. No longer do we have the continuing processes of oppressor and oppressed, but the final state of murderer and victim: a further and more decisive instance of what one had hoped to destroy.

From here, once the cycle is complete, one can see that Raskolnikov, and the theory by which he acts, are at the definitive point of consciousness of his age. The prospect looming here is of a society that interprets any threat to its values, aims and property—whether those threats be the lack of social progress, or the right of dispossession—as automatically a threat to its very existence. Yet it is *that* interpretation which is the real threat. While revolutionaries plot murder in the name of social progress, the forces of reaction, because identified with property, themselves conspire with the revolutionaries in what will necessarily be their own destruction should the revolution occur. For the fanatical, or for a crypto-revolutionary like Raskolnikov, if you can't have social progress then you prefer to have murder than nothing at all. And the victims, unknowingly, take their behaviour so far that they put themselves in a position where they will be murdered in order to retain their property. The result: human life is lost in the name of possessions and social progress; neither social progress is achieved nor property retained. What one has is murder by the rule.

Crime and Punishment and the Intelligentsia

Gary Saul Morson

Gary Saul Morson, professor of Slavic languages at Northwestern University in Evanston, Illinois, is among the most important contemporary critics of the works of Russian writers. His books on Tolstoy and Dostoyevsky are considered indispensable to critical understanding of those two authors. In the following article, Morson discusses *Crime and Punishment*'s lasting lesson for the educated classes of society. He argues that the novel is essentially a critique of the behavior and beliefs of members of the Russian intelligentsia, a term that Morson defines both in its present-day usage and in the way that Dostoyevsky used it. He concludes by comparing *Crime and Punishment* with Tolstoy's *War and Peace*, demonstrating that the attitudes of these two authors were not as different as literary criticism would make it seem.

Fyodor Dostoevsky's *Crime and Punishment* (1866) is above all a novel of ideas, and in its pages one reads about people who profess the philosophical obsessions of their time. In the characteristic manner of Russian literature, Dostoevsky focuses on the intelligentsia, its habits of thought, its delusions of insight, and its self-image of superiority to the rest of society. This novel, indeed, became a central text in the Russian debate about the intelligentsia's pretensions, and therefore came to speak to later generations as if it had just been published.

In fact, whenever an intelligentsia yields to a belief in its special mission to save society, Dostoevsky's criticisms achieve renewed relevance. Although his examples are Russian, his lessons are pertinent to many other cultures, including our own. . . .

Excerpted from Gary Saul Morson, "How to Read *Crime and Punishment*," *Commentary*, June 1992. Reprinted with permission; all rights reserved.

"Intelligentsia" is a word we get from Russian, where in the 19th century it meant something different from just the educated classes. An *intelligent* (member of the intelligentsia) was identified as such by his sense of solidarity with that group and by his contempt for all others, who were regarded either as enemies of the people or as benighted objects to be saved even against their will. *Intelligenty* were expected to live a particular kind of life—with the fastidiousness of the politically correct, they cultivated bad manners of a certain sort—and, above all, to share a set of approved ideas. Almost by definition, an *intelligent* believed in atheism (itself a sort of faith in Russia), socialism, and materialism. Somehow or other, from this materialist denial of all moral norms the intelligentsia managed to derive ethical urgency. As the philosopher Vladimir Soloviev quipped, the intelligentsia appeared to live according to an illogical syllogism: "Man has descended from the apes; *therefore* we should sacrifice ourselves for our fellow man."

Dostoevsky also stressed the tendency of the intelligentsia to transform everything into ideology and to take all ideas to a fanatical extreme; a Russian *intelligent*, he commented, is someone who can read Darwin on the survival of the fittest and promptly resolve to become a pickpocket. It need hardly be added that even petty theft could be justified as a contribution to the salvation of the people.

What was most important to the intelligentsia mentality was a mystique of revolution, specifically, revolution inspired and led by the intelligentsia itself. Members of the intelligentsia therefore held fast to a faith in two tenets: first, that they possessed or would soon find the underlying laws of history and civilization; and second, that by violent activity in accordance with those laws they could eliminate absolutely every evil from the world forever. A young man or woman who had never read a book but who accepted these revolutionary ideas, lived a properly sordid life, and belonged to an intelligentsia "circle" would be accepted as an *intelligent* much more readily than an intellectual like, let us say, Leo Tolstoy, who used his title of "Count," never conformed to reigning intellectual pieties, and lived on his estate, supremely disdainful of all those scribblers in the capital. Tolstoy in fact emerged as the key figure in a Russian countertradition, which answered the intelligentsia by developing an anti-ideological perspective that might be called "prosaics."

As it happened, this countertradition included most of Russia's greatest writers. The critic Mikhail Gershenzon did not much exaggerate when he observed that "in Russia an almost infallible gauge of an artist's genius is the extent of his hatred for the intelligentsia." Tolstoy's *War and Peace* became an exemplary text of the countertradition. That book repeatedly insists that there can be no viable "theory" of history and that people who act as if there were knowable historical laws rapidly become ineffective at everything except petty tyranny. For Tolstoy, history, like everything else in life, is shaped not primarily by dramatic events or noticeable crises but by the countless small events of daily life.

Anton Chekhov, too, was if anything even more devoted to the prosaic and even more contemptuous of "high drama" than Tolstoy. He expressed utter contempt for

> the indolent, lazily philosophizing cold [member of the] intelligentsia . . . who is not patriotic . . . who grumbles and negates everything, since for an idle mind it is easier to negate than affirm; who does not marry and refuses to educate his children. A flabby soul, flabby muscles, a lack of movement, inconsistent ideas—and all this on the strength of the fact that life has no meaning . . . and that money is an evil.

DOSTOEVSKY'S OTHER WORKS IN RELATION TO THE INTELLIGENTSIA

As for Dostoevsky, his position in the debate turned out to be remarkably complex. Himself a former radical who had been sentenced to mock-execution, a labor camp, and Siberian exile for his youthful political activities, Dostoevsky eventually became the great scourge of the intelligentsia. His novels chronicle the horror produced by this "vaudeville of demons," to use a phrase from *The Possessed* (a title more accurately rendered as *The Demons*). That novel catalogues the varieties of intelligentsia madness, and at least one of its characters, Shigalev, has earned Dostoevsky the reputation of prophet for his uncanny understanding of the totalitarianism that in Russia would eventually seize power.

For Dostoevsky, nothing leads to greater evil than schemes to end evil once and for all. And yet he himself was drawn to such schemes. He seemed to oscillate between opposite responses to the intelligentsia. At times, he rejected ideology altogether and, like Tolstoy and Chekhov, turned to the prosaic virtues. But at other times, he argued that the intelligentsia was right in its yearnings for the millennium; it had simply put its faith in the wrong source of salvation. The answer was to be found not in materialism but in religion, not in populist or Marxist socialism but in what Dostoevsky called the "Christian socialism" of Russian Orthodoxy.

In his most "possessed" writings, Dostoevsky asserted—quite literally—that he had ascertained the date at which the world would come to an end and the Kingdom of God would be established on earth. His insight as an artist had, he wrote, allowed him to see the inner workings of Providence and to read the plot of history as he could read the plot of a novel. These prophecies—they were not just predictions—occur in *The Diary of a Writer*, which contains article after article devoted to explaining world politics in terms of the biblical Book of Revelation. In its Russian Orthodox version, this kind of thinking led straight to fanatical anti-Semitism, and indeed Dostoevsky's truly horrifying anti-Semitic writings date from this period of his life.

In earlier passages of *The Diary of a Writer*, however, Dostoevsky rejects millenarian thinking in favor of a prosaic viewpoint. Insisting on the need for skepticism, he mocks both the intelligentsia's habit of discovering "laws" of history and its pretensions to save mankind "at a stroke." In one memorable passage, Dostoevsky contrasts grandiose plans to liberate all humanity with the efforts of a certain "humble and little fellow" who spent a lifetime saving money so that, every ten years, he could buy the freedom of a single serf. By the end of his life, Dostoevsky reports, this unknown man had liberated three or four people. Dostoevsky then imagines the sarcasm that *intelligenty* would direct at such a quixotic project; but he insists that it is just such "microscopic efforts" that do the most good and constitute the greatest heroism.

When his prophecy of the End failed, Dostoevsky returned to this prosaic standpoint. In *The Brothers Karamazov*, his last novel, the wise elder Zossima tells the story of a man who fabricates "enthusiastic schemes for the service of humanity" but cannot share a room with someone for two days without hating him. And yet, this man concludes, "it has always happened that the more I detest men individually the more ardent becomes my love for humanity [in general]." Zossima instructs that real love must be for real, individual people.

A CONFLICTED INTELLIGENT

Like Dostoevsky's thought as a whole, *Crime and Punishment* seems torn between these two competing alternatives to the mentality of the intelligentsia. It is almost as if there were two novels here, sharing a diagnosis but prescribing incompatible cures.

Crime and Punishment clearly offers an analysis, if not an etiology, of the intelligentsia's sick mentality, as the novel's original reviewers recognized. The novel's hero, Raskolnikov ("the schismatic"), "had entirely given up attending to his daily affairs and did not want to attend to them." He has ceased earning money as a tutor, refuses to worry about such "commonplace trifles" as paying his rent, and does nothing but lie on his threadbare couch or aimlessly wander the streets. "To become more degraded and slovenly would have been difficult; but Raskolnikov even enjoyed it in his present state of mind." People who see this self-absorbed youth on the street take him to be drunk.

In a letter to his publisher, Dostoevsky explained that his hero had succumbed to "an infirmity of notions . . . under the influence of those strange, 'incomplete' ideas which go floating about in the air." The more Raskolnikov neglects his daily affairs, the greater the hold those ideas have on him. Yet these "incomplete" theories contradict each other, and later, when Raskolnikov tries to explain to himself and others what has guided his behavior, he recognizes that none of them suffices. Nevertheless, they all converge on a single action: murdering an old woman, a pawnbroker.

One of Raskolnikov's theories demands this murder on moral grounds. Kill her and give her money to the poor; "one death for hundreds of lives—it's simple arithmetic!" Another theory denies the existence of morality altogether. Good and evil are simply prejudices, "artificial terrors" inherited from religion, which means that, for the man who truly dares to transgress, "all is permitted." Indeed, Raskolnikov imagines that all the great men of history, from Solon to Napoleon, acted on precisely this principle, which justifies any crime if for no other reason than that there is no such thing as crime.

What is remarkable about the "Napoleonic" theory is that it distills the intelligentsia mentality to its pure form. Usually terrorists and revolutionaries assert that their theories and actions will save humanity, and *therefore* that the intelligentsia is society's vanguard. The middle step of the argument, the aspiration to rectify social evil, is what justifies the claim to superiority over ordinary people. Raskolnikov is honest enough to do away with this middle step and go directly to the claim of superiority, which is the constant element preserved through all ideological fashions.

And yet, even this theory does not explain why Raskolnikov commits his crime. Later he admits that he always knew he was not a Napoleon, that he was not one of the geniuses with "the right to transgress." Can one imagine Napoleon groping with shaking hands under an old woman's bed while terrified at the sight of her blood?, he asks himself. Can one even imagine Napoleon first needing to invent a theory before doing what he had to do? No, a true Napoleon would have killed "without casuistry."

In that case, what *is* Raskolnikov's motive? This question perplexes him almost from the moment he commits the murder, and he never resolves it. Apparently, Dostoevsky also remained uncertain, and his notebooks record his own quest for a motive, which seems to parallel his hero's. Dostoevsky recognized that the portrait of Raskolnikov was true—his keen psychological sense told him that—but he did not know why. Critics from then until now have remained just as convinced of the book's psychological accuracy and just as unconvincing in identifying Raskolnikov's underlying motive.

A Contrary Position: Tolstoy on *Crime and Punishment*

As it happens, the most persuasive answer has come not from a professional critic but from Leo Tolstoy. In Tolstoy's view, there is no "underlying motive" for Raskolnikov's crime, no single moment in which he "decides" on murder. Rather, the crime emerges from the climate of Raskolnikov's mind, which is itself the product of countless small decisions made at many ordinary moments. Tolstoy alludes to several passages in which the novel tells us that although Raskolnikov constantly teases himself with the possibility of murder, "never for a single moment during the whole time could he believe in the feasibility of his designs." Raskolnikov talks to himself, lies on his couch daydreaming, or toys with some odd detail of his scheme, but he neither chooses nor ever renounces his terrible plan.

Tolstoy regards passages like these as fully revealing. The

idea of murder is never anything but a dream for Raskolnikov, a mere possibility, even when he stands before the old woman, ax in hand. That is why he never actively prepares himself for the crime, only doing the bare minimum to prove to himself that he has not repudiated it. But when a unique opportunity arises, that "minimum" turns out to be quite enough for the dream to become reality. It leads him to the murder scene, where he must act even without actually having made a decision to act.

In Tolstoy's view, this is precisely how important decisions are often "made." It is not a single moment, but the whole way Raskolnikov thinks and lives, what Tolstoy calls his "true life," that ends in murder:

> That question was decided . . . when he was doing nothing, and was only thinking, when only his consciousness was active: and in that consciousness tiny, tiny alterations were taking place. . . . Tiny, tiny alterations—but on them depend the most immense and terrible consequences.

Not grand events, but those "tiny, tiny alterations," are what make a life good or bad. Tolstoy's own novels focus on such "tiny, tiny alterations," into which he divides even the simplest and most apparently indivisible actions. (That is one reason his books are so long.)

In those restless hours when Raskolnikov is torn between renouncing and yielding to his murderous plan, he is amazed to find himself going to his friend Razumikhin. Like the simple decent maid Nastasya, who brings food to Raskolnikov at her own expense, Razumikhin conveys cheerfulness and sociability; he is never discouraged by setbacks, and, though poor, is resourceful at getting odd jobs. Throughout the novel, he also serves as Dostoevsky's mouthpiece for criticizing all grand theorizing, as he insists on the messiness of history and the need for individual responsibility in an uncertain world. He directs his sarcasm toward all attempts to gain a fortune or solve social problems without steady, persistent effort, and mocks the idea that "a social system, coming out of some mathematical head, will at once organize the whole of mankind and instantly make it righteous and sinless, sooner than any living process." Going to Razumikhin thus indicates a desire to escape from the mentality leading to crime, and in the novel as a whole, Razumikhin—his name means "the reasonable one"—most clearly carries the prosaic idea.

If Nastasya and Razumikhin speak prosaic truths, one character, the detective Porfiry Petrovich, actually seems to have read Tolstoy. As it happens, *Crime and Punishment* and *War and Peace* were being serialized in the same "thick journal" at the same time—such was the intensity of literary creativity in Russia in the 1860's and 1870's—and so an interesting dialogue between the two great novels became possible. Most obviously, both seem engaged in a debate about "the idea of Napoleon." Thus, explaining to Raskolnikov why he does not follow established police procedure, Porfiry Petrovich claims that procedures, like theories, are made only for the idealized situation, whereas "every crime as soon as it actually occurs turns into a completely particular case, unlike all the previous ones." As an example, Porfiry adduces

> the former Austrian *Hofkriegrat*. . . . On paper, they had Napoleon crushed and taken prisoner, it was all worked out and arranged in the cleverest manner in their study, and then, lo and behold, General Mack surrenders with his entire army!

Porfiry doubtless derived this striking example from a recently published section of *War and Peace*, where it illustrates that there can be no science of war (or history) because an infinitude of contingencies, choices, and "tiny alterations" of circumstance render each military or historical situation irreducibly particular. Tolstoy's wisest general, Kutuzov, understands it is not advance strategies but attentiveness to the flux of unforeseeable particularities that makes the difference; and Dostoevsky's detective applies this lesson to civilian life. He makes himself into the Kutuzov of crime.

CHRISTIANITY AS AN ALTERNATIVE PERSPECTIVE

Until well into *Crime and Punishment*, then, prosaic attentiveness and responsibility oppose the abstraction and megalomania of the intelligentsia. But for temperamental reasons, Dostoevsky apparently grew dissatisfied with the prosaic answer. Without revising the novel as a whole, he added a second alternative, the Christian myth. He changed Sonia, the prostitute who reads the Gospel to Raskolnikov and eventually follows him to Siberia, from the realistic and partly flawed person she was in his notebooks to the pure and perfectly Christian symbol of wisdom—as the diminutive of Sophia, the name Sonia means "wisdom"—she became in the published version. This violation of the realistic tenor of the novel was evidently quite deliberate, but readers have nonetheless often deemed it a flaw.

Readers have been still more disturbed by the novel's epilogue in which Raskolnikov is at last converted from Napoleon to Sonia, from ideology to wisdom. The epilogue completely abandons the realistic tenor of the work, and we enter mythic, if not biblical, time. Raskolnikov finds faith while contemplating nomads on an eternal landscape where "time itself seemed to stop, as if the centuries of Abraham and his flock had not passed." No meticulously detailed psychological process accounts for his conversion; a mythic dream, and an implicit appeal to the reader's own longing for faith, bring the novel to its Christian close.

Summoned as it were by professional duty, generations of scholars have identified numerous connections between the epilogue and the rest of the novel. But the very need for such a persistent defense testifies to the dissatisfaction readers usually feel. Most have agreed with Philip Rahv, who described Sonia's "answer" and the novel's epilogue as "implausible and out of key with the work as a whole."

The problem, I think, is not that a Christian solution could not have been made to work aesthetically, but that the novel never reconciles its prosaic and its mythic impulses. The result is a confusion of two designs. Or we might put it this way: the author's final intention conflicts with what might be called the energy of the work as it unfolds. Sensing the prosaic energy that drives the novel forward, the reader feels cheated by an intention that does not seem to emerge from the whole. The indisputable fact that *Crime and Punishment* is still one of the world's greatest masterpieces testifies to the amazing power of Dostoevsky's conflicted genius.

Ideas and Doubles

Ernest Simmons

Ernest Simmons is the author of a number of land-
mark studies about Russian writers of the nineteenth
century, including *Dostoevsky: The Making of a Novelist*. Here he writes about what sets Dostoyevsky
apart from the other giants of Russian literature. Unlike Pushkin, Tolstoy, or Gogol—the three major authors who precede or are contemporaries of Dostoyevsky—Simmons sees Dostoyevsky's insistence on
making his characters represent philosophical ideas
as a radical innovation.

In this selection, Simmons looks at the character
of Raskolnikov in terms of the idea of dualism, or
"doubles." Simmons makes the claim that the duality
with which Dostoyevsky creates Raskolnikov was
not only what enabled him to depict the workings of
the mind of a murderer, but also caused him to have
to reevaluate his own beliefs about human nature.

In the series of celebrated novels beginning with *Crime and
Punishment* (1866), Dostoevsky stressed a feature that had
been only hinted at in his earlier writings and was new in
Russian and European fiction in general. Ideas now began to
play the central role in his novels. His chief figures are often
embodied ideas and he appears to be concerned not so much
with the life of his characters as with the ideas they represent. Such a process, of course, leads to the disintegration of
the ordinary world of the novel and in its place we have a
world of men and women organized according to the ideas
that possess them. The characters have no biography, for
they are exempt from the cause and effect of daily life and the
only verisimilitude is their inner word about themselves.

In Russia in the 1920's excellent critical studies were devoted to the significance of ideas in the structural complex of
Dostoevsky's fiction, but all were agreed that he wrote not

Excerpted from Ernest Simmons, *Introduction to Russian Realism*. Copyright ©1965
by Indiana University Press. Reprinted by permission of Indiana University Press.

philosophical or purpose novels, but rather novels about ideas. The essential conflict in these investigations was whether Dostoevsky synthesized the ideas of his characters into a philosophical position of his own or whether he refrained from resolving their conflicting ideas, allowing them to coexist as a perpetual dramatization of the internal contradictions of man. In the latter case the assumption would be that the hero was given complete freedom to develop his ideas because Dostoevsky was not interested in him as a typification of a way of life, as an object of reality, but only as a special point of view on the world and on himself.

If these scholars had been able to make full use of Dostoevsky's notebooks, letters, and journalistic writings, the extent of his conscious control over the characters and ideas they embody would have been much clarified. To be sure, the character's integrity and self-awareness of ideas deriving from his total personality are always artistically sustained, but it is a mistake to imagine that Dostoevsky did not consciously work out in advance a concrete system of thought for a major character, although he may have elaborated the plan set down in his notebooks and letters in the course of writing the novel.

WHAT THE NOTEBOOKS SAY

For example, in the notebooks and in letters to his publisher Katkov, Dostoevsky provides us with a comprehensive outline of *Crime and Punishment* and much information about the nature of Raskolnikov and the basic ideas he embodies. He wishes to present his hero at the moment of the birth of a terribly destructive idea which is the fruit of his rebellion against society. Raskolnikov's theory of ordinary and extraordinary people and the crime that results from it are products of what Dostoevsky considered the distorted thinking of the young revolutionary-minded generation. They are people who think it possible to organize a social system on a rational plan, that reason can take the place of human nature, of the living process of life. In his journalistic writings, as well as in *Notes from the Underground*, Dostoevsky had already expressed a negative position on these claims which he associated with the pretensions of socialism, for he believed that life would not submit to mechanical rules or the living soul to logic. This is the central idea of *Crime and Punishment*—to portray a man who is the victim of "incomplete ideas" going the rounds, as he explained in his letter to Katkov, a person who tries to order his life on a self-willed plan of reason. In addition, Dostoevsky further explains to his publisher, he wants to demonstrate through his hero that the legal punishment inflicted for a crime intimidates a criminal infinitely less than lawmakers think, partly because the guilty person morally demands punishment.

In the notebooks as Dostoevsky analyzes the idea in terms of the hero, he recognizes a persistent ambiguity deriving from the dualism of Raskolnikov whom he has cast as one of his thinking Doubles. Of this there can be no doubt. In the novel Razumikhin says of his friend Raskolnikov: "In truth, it is as though he were alternating between two opposing characters." And a striking jotting in the notebook not only identifies the fact of dualism in the characterization, but also reflects Dostoevsky's image of the Doubles as containing the opposing traits of two other character types—the Meek and the Self-Willed. For he writes: "Svidrigailov is desperation, the most cynical. Sonya is hope, the most unrealizable. (These must be expressed by Raskolnikov himself.) He is passionately attached to them both."

It is the inner contradiction of self-will and submissiveness in Raskolnikov's nature which, when expressed in action, creates the intense drama of the novel. This dualism undermines his self-willed theory of murder and in the end leaves him completely confused about his motive for killing the old pawnbroker—a miracle of psychological perception on Dostoevsky's part. And after the murder Raskolnikov is similarly torn between Sonya's path of submissiveness to expiation of his crime and his self-willed pride which convinces him that the murder was a crime only because he failed in his purpose.

HOW THE "DOUBLES" CHANGED DOSTOEVSKY'S MIND

Interestingly enough, the notebooks indicate that Dostoevsky, having originally launched his hero with a single-minded motive for committing the murder, also got momentarily lost in Raskolnikov's dualistic crosspurposes. In a fragment of dialogue in the notes Raskolnikov argues a specific motivation for the crime: "There is one law—a moral law. Agreed, agreed! Well, sir, and this law? Why, if conscience does not accuse me, I seize authority, I acquire power—whether money or might, and not for evil. I bring

DOSTOYEVSKY'S FIRST "DOUBLE"

*In 1846, Dostoyevsky published his second book, a novel
entitled* The Double. *This work contains many of the
themes found in* Crime and Punishment, *most notably that of a
character who has a "double" in the world. A major difference is
that the double that haunts the main character, Golyadkin (his
name means "naked") is presented either as the product of insanity or perhaps even something supernatural. In this excerpt
from the novel, Golyadkin sees his double.*

Mr. Golyadkin caught his breath. The stranger stopped exactly
before the house in which Mr. Golyadkin lodged. He heard a
ring at the bell and almost at the same time the grating of the
iron bolt. The gate opened, the stranger stooped, darted in and
disappeared. Almost at the same instant Mr. Golyadkin reached
the spot and like an arrow flew in at the gate. Heedless of the
grumbling porter, he ran, gasping for breath, into the yard, and
immediately saw his interesting companion, whom he had lost
sight of for a moment.

The stranger darted towards the staircase which led to Mr.
Golyadkin's flat. Mr. Golyadkin rushed after him. The stairs
were dark, damp and dirty. At every turning there were
heaped-up masses of refuse from the flats, so that any unac-
customed stranger who found himself on the stairs in the dark
was forced to travel to and fro for half an hour in danger of
breaking his legs, cursing the stairs as well as the friends who
lived in such an inconvenient place. But Mr. Golyadkin's companion seemed as though familiar with it, as though at home;

---

happiness. Well, then, because of a paltry screen, to stand and
look over to that side of the screen, to envy and hate and to
stand still. That's ignoble." On the margin, opposite the passage, Dostoevsky wrote: "Devil take it! This is partly right."

Similarly, Raskolnikov's arguments for and against revealing his crime and accepting punishment obviously began to
raise doubts in Dostoevsky's mind that the denouement
which he had long since conveyed to his publisher was the
artistically logical one. Entries in the notebooks show his
fluctuations on this score. Should Raskolnikov, a facet of
whose nature is endowed with satanic pride, seek the way
out of suicide, the only possible solution of the wholly self-
willed character Svidrigailov? And under the heading "Conclusion for the novel," Dostoevsky set down in one of the
notebooks: "Raskolnikov goes to shoot himself." But in the

he ran up lightly, without difficulty, showing a perfect knowledge of his surroundings. Mr. Golyadkin had almost caught him up; in fact, once or twice the stranger's coat flicked him on the nose. His heart stood still. The stranger stopped before the door of Mr. Golyadkin's flat, knocked on it, and (which would, however, have surprised Mr. Golyadkin at any other time) Petrushka, as though he had been sitting up in expectation, opened the door at once and, with a candle in his hand, followed the strange as the latter went in. The hero of our story dashed into his lodging beside himself; without taking off his hat or coat he crossed the little passage and stood still in the doorway of his room, as though thunderstruck. All his presentiments had come true. All that he had dreaded and surmised was coming to pass in reality. His breath failed him, his head was in a whirl. The stranger, also in his coat and hat, was sitting before him on his bed, and with a faint smile, screwing up his eyes, nodded to him in a friendly way. Mr. Golyadkin wanted to scream, but could not—to protest in some way, but his strength failed him. His hair stood on end, and he almost fell down with horror. And, indeed, there was good reason. He recognised his nocturnal visitor. The nocturnal visitor was no other than himself—Mr. Golyadkin himself, another Mr. Golyadkin, but absolutely the same as himself—in fact, what is called a double in every respect.

Excerpted from Fyodor Dostoyevsky, *The Double* (translated by Constance Garnett) in *The Short Novels of Dostoevsky.* New York: Dial Press, 1945, pp. 475–615 (this selection from 514–15). Full text also available online at www.maths.nott.ac.uk/personal/pmyjaw/Dostoevsky2/texts.html.

end Dostoevsky sacrificed this aesthetically satisfying conclusion to the original idea of the novel which was his own idea rather than that of his hero—Raskolnikov must reveal his crime, accept his punishment, and having discovered faith in Christ, will learn in prison that happiness cannot be achieved by a reasoned plan of existence but must be earned through suffering. Dostoevsky had applied the balm, salvation by suffering, which he had learned in his own prison experience, to resolve the dualism of his hero and dissipate the dangerous "incomplete ideas" which had led him to crime as, in a sense, they had once led Dostoevsky to commit a crime against the state. It is a most lame and impotent conclusion.

From this point on the remaining novels reveal a pattern of uniformity in dramatized ideas, type characters, and Dostoevskian philosophy cast against a background of extraordinary diversity of action. There is no lack of individualization in heroes and heroines, but increasingly all reality becomes only an element in their self-knowledge. As in the case of *Crime and Punishment* at the end, the other masterpieces irresistibly reach out more and more to the chief question that consciously or unconsciously profoundly troubled Dostoevsky's mind—the existence of God.

CHRONOLOGY

First names and patronymics (where necessary to differentiate between two individuals with the same first name) are used instead of the family name.

1819

Mikhail Andreyevich Dostoyevsky, a thirty-year-old physician, marries Marya Fyodorovna Nechayeva, a nineteen-year-old merchant's daughter.

1820

The Dostoyevskys' first son, Mikhail Mikhailovich, is born.

1821

Fyodor Mikhailovich Dostoyevsky born in Moscow on October 30.

1822

Varvara Mikhailovna Dostoyevskaya is born.

1825

Andrey Mikhailovich Dostoyevsky is born; Czar Alexander I dies; the "Decembrist" revolt occurs; Czar Nicholas I ascends after the revolts are suppressed.

1829

Vera Mikhailovna and Lyubov Mikhailovna Dostoyevskaya are born; Lyubov dies a few days later.

1831

Nikolai Mikhailovich Dostoyevsky born; Dostoyevsky family acquires the Daravoe village, where they would spend subsequent summers.

1833–37

Mikhail and Fyodor are sent to various boarding schools in Moscow.

1835

Alexandra Mikhailovna Dostoyevskaya born.

1837

Marya Fyodorovna dies of tuberculosis and exhaustion; Alexander Pushkin, Russian preeminent writer of the time, dies after being shot in a duel; Fyodor and his older brother are sent to a preparatory academy in St. Petersburg.

1838

Fyodor gains admission into the Academy of Military Engineers; Mikhail is refused admission, and eventually moves to Tallinn, Estonia.

1839

Mikhail Andreyevich dies under mysterious circumstances at Daravoe.

1840

Varvara marries Peter Andreyevich Karepin, a wealthy landowner.

1842

Mikhail marries Emilya Fyodorovna von Ditmar.

1843

Fyodor graduates from the Academy and works on translations from French.

1844

Fyodor refuses his army commission to devote himself to writing.

1845

Fyodor meets and becomes friends with the noted critic Vissarion Belinsky and other important figures of Russian literature.

1846

Fyodor publishes *Poor Folk, The Double,* and *Mr. Prokharchin* and meets Mikhail Vasilievich Butashevich-Petrashevsky, in whose intellectual "circles" he begins to take part.

1848

Fyodor publishes numerous short stories.

1849

Netochka Nezvanova is published. Fyodor and Mikhail are arrested and Fyodor is sentenced to death for his activities in the Petrashevsky circle. His sentence is commuted to four years' imprisonment instead, but not before he is brought before a firing squad.

1850–54

Fyodor serves his sentence in a penal camp in Omsk, in Siberia.

1854–59

Fyodor is forced to serve in the military in Semipalatinsk in the southern Siberian steppes. Here he meets Baron Vrangel and Marya Dmitrievna Isaeva.

1857

Fyodor marries Marya Dmitrievna.

1859

Fyodor is allowed to resign from the army; he and Marya move to Tver in summer and then to Petersburg in December.

1860

Along with his brother Mikhail, Fyodor founds the journal *Vremya (Time)* and publishes the first part of *The House of the Dead.*

1861

Fyodor publishes *The Insulted and the Injured.*

1862

Fyodor takes a trip to Western Europe and begins his lengthy romantic involvement with Apollinarya (Polina) Suslova; the remainder of *The House of the Dead* and *A Nasty Tale* are published.

1863

Time banned by government; *Winter Notes on Summer Impressions* is published.

1864

Mikhail and Fyodor start *Epoch* as a replacement for *Time; Notes from Underground* is published; Marya Dmitrievna dies in April of tuberculosis; Mikhail Mikhailovich dies in July of exhaustion.

1865

Fyodor travels in Europe again and his proposals for marriage are declined by several women, including Polina Suslova.

1866

Fyodor publishes *Crime and Punishment* and *The Gambler* and meets Anna Grigorievna Snitkina, a nineteen-year-old stenographer who helps him finish the latter work in time to meet his publisher's deadline.

1867

Fyodor and Anna are married and leave Russia for four years, primarily residing in Germany, Switzerland, and Italy.

1868

Sofia Fyodorovna Dostoyevskaya is born in Geneva and dies three months later; *The Idiot* is published.

1869

Lyubov Fyodorovna Dostoyevskaya is born in Dresden; Fyodor begins work on a massive project he planned to call *The Life of a Great Sinner.*

1870

The Eternal Husband is published.

1871

The Dostoyevskys return to Russia; *The Devils* (a.k.a. *The Possessed* or *Demons)* begins serial publication; Fyodor Fyodorovich Dostoyevsky is born.

1873

Fyodor takes over editorship of *The Citizen,* and *The Diary of a Writer,* his column, becomes a regular feature; *Bobok* is published

1875

A Raw Youth is published; Alyosha Fyodorovich Dostoyevsky is born.

1876

The Diary of a Writer becomes its own journal, under Fyodor's sole editorship.

1877

The Dream of a Ridiculous Man is published; Anna Dostoyevskaya collects and issues *The Diary of a Writer* in a book edition.

1878

Alyosha dies of epilepsy; Fyodor seeks the solace of Father Ambrose, an Orthodox monk.

1879–80

Serial publication of *The Brothers Karamazov.*

1880

Delivers a memorable speech at the inauguration of a statue of Pushkin in Moscow.

1881

Dies of emphysema on January 28 (February 9) and is buried at the monastery of St. Alexander Nevsky in Petersburg; Tsar Alexander II is assassinated a month later.

1918

Anna Dostoyevskaya dies in the Crimea.

FOR FURTHER RESEARCH

WORKS BY DOSTOYEVSKY READILY AVAILABLE IN ENGLISH TRANSLATION

An Accidental Family (a.k.a. *A Raw Youth;* tr. by Richard Freeborn). Oxford, England: Oxford University Press, 1994.

The Best Short Stories of Dostoyevsky (tr. by David Magarshack). New York: Modern Library, 1992.

"Bobok" in *The Eternal Husband and Other Stories* (tr. by Richard Pevear and Larissa Volokhonsky). New York: Bantam, 1997.

The Brothers Karamazov (critical edition, tr. by Jessie Coulson). New York: Norton, 1976.

The Complete Letters of Fyodor Dostoyevsky. Ann Arbor, MI: Ardis, 1988–1991.

Crime and Punishment (critical edition, tr. by Jessie Coulson). Norton: New York, 1989.

The Crocodile (tr. by Samuel D. Cioran). Ann Arbor, MI: Ardis, 1985.

Demons: A Novel in Three Parts (a.k.a. *The Devils,* or *The Possessed;* tr. by Richard Pevear and Larissa Volokhonsky). New York: Knopf, 1995.

A Diary of a Writer (tr. by Kenneth Lantz). Evanston, IL: Northwestern University Press, 1997.

The Double. New York: Dover Books, 1997.

"The Dream of a Ridiculous Man" in *The Eternal Husband and Other Stories* (tr. by Richard Pevear and Larissa Volokhonsky). New York: Bantam, 1997.

The Eternal Husband and Other Stories (tr. by Richard Pevear and Larissa Volokhonsky). New York: Bantam, 1997.

The Gambler (tr. by Andrew R. MacAndrew). New York: Norton, 1997.

The House of the Dead (tr. by David McDuff). New York: Viking Penguin, 1986.

The Idiot (tr. by David Magarshack). New York: Penguin, 1956.

The Insulted and the Injured (tr. by Constance Garnett). Westport, CT: Greenwood Press, 1985.

"The Meek One" in *The Eternal Husband and Other Stories* (tr. by Richard Pevear and Larissa Volokhonsky). New York: Bantam, 1997.

"A Nasty Tale" in *The Eternal Husband and Other Stories* (tr. by Richard Pevear and Larissa Volokhonsky). New York: Bantam, 1997.

Netochka Nezvanova (tr. by Jane Kentish). New York: Penguin, 1986.

Notes from Underground (critical ed., tr. by Michael R. Katz). New York: Norton, 1989.

Poor Folk (tr. by David R. McDuff). New York: Viking Penguin, 1989.

Uncle's Dream in *The Short Novels of Dostoevsky*. New York: Dial Press, 1946.

The Village of Stepanchikovo and Its Inhabitants (tr. by Ignat Avsey). New York: Viking Penguin, 1995.

Winter Notes on Summer Impressions (tr. by David Patterson). Evanston, IL: Northwestern University Press, 1997.

FOR FURTHER RESEARCH

Harold Bloom, ed., *Modern Critical Interpretations: Fyodor Dostoyevsky's* Crime and Punishment. New York: Chelsea House, 1988.

Richard L. Chapple, *A Dostoevsky Dictionary*. Ann Arbor, MI: Ardis, 1983.

Peter J. Conradi, *Fyodor Dostoevsky*. New York: St. Martin's Press, 1988.

Gary Cox, *Crime and Punishment: A Mind to Murder*. Boston: Twayne, 1990.

Anna Dostoyevskaya, *Dostoevsky Portrayed by His Wife; the Diary and Reminiscences of Mme. Dostoevsky* (ed. by S.S. Koteliansky). London: Routledge, 1926.

Robert Louis Jackson, ed., *Twentieth Century Interpretations of* Crime and Punishment: *A Collection of Critical Essays.* Englewood Cliffs, NJ: Prentice-Hall, 1974.

Leslie A. Johnson, *The Experience of Time in* Crime and Punishment. Columbus, OH: Slavica, 1985.

Charles E. Passage, *Character Names in Dostoyevsky's Fiction.* Ann Arbor, MI: Ardis, 1982.

Richard Arthur Peace, *Dostoyevsky: An Examination of the Major Novels.* Cambridge, England: Cambridge University Press, 1971.

Victor Terras, *F.M. Dostoevsky: Life, Work, and Criticism.* Fredericton, Canada: York Press, 1984.

Edward Wasiolek, ed., *The Notebooks for* Crime and Punishment. Chicago: University of Chicago Press, 1967.

Rene Wellek, ed., *Dostoevsky: A Collection of Critical Essays.* Englewood Cliffs, NJ: Prentice-Hall, 1964.

BIOGRAPHIES OF DOSTOYEVSKY

Alba Amoia, *Feodor Dostoevsky.* New York: Continuum, 1993.

Joseph Frank, *Dostoevsky* (4 vols.). Princeton, NJ: Princeton University Press, 1976–1995.

Geir Kjetsaa, *Fyodor Dostoyevsky, A Writer's Life.* New York: Viking, 1987.

David Magarshack, *Dostoevsky.* New York: Harcourt, Brace and World, 1962.

Konstantin Molchulsky, *Dostoyevsky: His Life and Work.* Princeton, NJ: Princeton University Press, 1971.

Henri Troyat, *Firebrand: The Life of Dostoevsky.* New York: Roy Publishers, 1946.

CHRONOLOGICAL LIST OF DOSTOYEVSKY'S PUBLICATIONS

Poor Folk (1846)

The Double (1846)

Mr. Prokharchin (1846)

A Novel in Nine Letters (1847)

The Landlady (1847)

The Stranger-Woman (1848)

A Weak Heart (1848)

Polzunkov (1848)

An Honest Thief (1848)

A Jealous Husband (1848)

A Christmas Tree and a Wedding (1848)

White Nights (1848)

Netochka Nezvanova (1849)

A Little Hero (1849)

Uncle's Dream (1859)

The Village of Stepanchikovo and Its Inhabitants (1859)

The House of the Dead (1860–1862)

The Insulted and the Injured (1861)

An Unpleasant Predicament (1861)

A Silly Story (1861)

A Nasty Tale (1862)

Winter Notes on Summer Impressions (1863)

Notes From Underground (1864)

An Unusual Happening (1865)

The Crocodile (1865)

Crime and Punishment (1866)

The Gambler (1866)

The Idiot (1868)

The Eternal Husband (1870)

The Devils [or *The Possessed,* or *Demons*] (1871–1872)

Bobok (1873)

A Raw Youth [or *The Adolescent,* or *An Accidental Family*] (1875)

A Gentle Creature (1876)

The Dream of a Ridiculous Man (1877)

A Diary of a Writer (1877)

The Brothers Karamazov (1879–1880)

INDEX